# ice cream
# SUNDAE

## 100 GREATEST FOUNTAIN FORMULAS

# ice cream
# SUNDAE

## 100 GREATEST FOUNTAIN FORMULAS

by Michael Turback

## COPYRIGHT NOTICE

# simple sundae instructions

### step 1
*Select a clean sundae dish that isn't cracked or chipped, and hold the dish between your fingers and close to the bottom of the bowl.*

### step 2
*Pour a small portion of topping into the bottom of the dish.
This adds to eye appeal and eating quality.*

### step 3
*Add one scoop of ice cream. Then put another scoop
of ice cream on top of the first scoop.*

### step 4
*Cover the ice cream with the larger portion of topping.*

### step 5
*If you're making a nut sundae, cover the entire surface of the ice cream.
Dry nuts should be sprinkled with spoon and nuts in syrup should
be ladled carefully so the mixture doesn't overflow.*

### step 6
*Add whipped cream.*

### step 7
*Decorate with garnish.*

# anatomy of a sundae

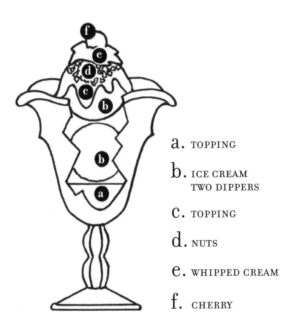

a. TOPPING

b. ICE CREAM
TWO DIPPERS

c. TOPPING

d. NUTS

e. WHIPPED CREAM

f. CHERRY

"In these harsh and uncertain times, as the establishment cracks and institutions crumble, it is no wonder we reach out to ice cream. It is a link to innocence and security, healing, soothing, wholesome... the last of the eternal verities."

*New York Magazine* restaurant critic Gael Green wrote those words on August 3, 1970, during economic recession and painful ending of the Vietnam War. Nearly 40 years later, as we struggle with the mess at hand, this book encourages you to hold that thought.

# introduction

Sundaes are us, and they have been pleasuring our collective senses ever since 1892, when an enterprising Ithaca, New York, soda fountain proprietor accessorized a scoop of ice cream with sweet syrup and candied cherry, then named it after the Sabbath.

A sundae is not just any dish, but a confection that is original, enduring, and authentically American. For well over a century, the ice cream sundae has been a symbol of our abundance and appetite, our ingenuity, and our never-lost youth.

In their assembly, sundaes provide unrestrained opportunities to express our essential character. They acquire personality not only through their combination of ingredients, but through the history they witness.

During the twists and turns our country has taken over the past hundred or so years, ice cream sundaes have been standing by to lift our spirits. After the 1929 stock market crash, one of the few luxuries that average folks could afford was the democratically-priced sundae. During World War II, patriotic "Victory Sundaes" included a Defense Saving Stamp with every purchase, while the Navy commissioned floating ice cream parlors (refrigerated barges with ice cream plants) to boost troop morale. In wartime and in hard times, home refrigerators were stocked with ice creams that, with a dash of imagination, provided the basis for an irresistible sundae.

Following the classic model, sundaes are served in footed, tulip shaped glasses, filled with scoops of ice cream as the foundation for interplays of sauces or syrups, perhaps the crunch of nuts, and often a cloud of whipped cream and signature cherry. Yet it was Somerset Maugham who wrote, "Tradition is a guide and not a jailer," and that explains our unremitting playfulness with sundae formulas over the years.

As the first decade of the twenty-first century draws to a close, it seems an appropriate time to provide a scholarly glimpse into fountain culture. From humble, forgotten relics to dishes that have become popular standards, 100 essential sundaes have been arranged in alphabetical order so that they may be instantly accessible.

But this is more than just a collection of recipes. I like to think of it as a culinary adventure story, with an ice cream dessert as the central character. On every page there is a scoop of history, a measure of technique, and a sprinkle of trivia, all in aid of explaining the unique Americaness of the ice cream sundae.

Michael Turback
*www.icecreamsundae.com*

# all-american sundae

Puzzling over how to mix business with patriotism in wartime 1942, the Ice Cream Merchandising Institute, a promotional arm of the dairy industry, created a "Victory Sundae" advertising campaign. Participating merchants included a Defense Savings Stamp with every sundae sold. The slogan was "Keep "Em Buying to Keep 'Em Flying," and the most fashionable sundae colors were red, white, and blue.

**4 ounces** marshmallow syrup
**2 scoops** vanilla ice cream
**1 tablespoon** crushed maraschino cherries
**1 tablespoon** blueberries

Into a tulip sundae glass put 1 ounce marshmallow syrup. Add 2 scoops of vanilla ice cream. Cover with remaining marshmallow. Spoon cherries on one side of the glass, blueberries on the opposite side, leaving a white stripe down the middle.

{ During World War II, Secretary of the Navy James Forrestal commi sioned floating refrigerated barges for the manufacture of ice cream to serve troops in the Pacific. }

*The Washington House Hotel in Two Rivers, Wisconsin, filled with relics from the old Ed Berner's soda fountain, creates a version of this World War II formula called the Washington House Sundae.*

# american beauty sundae

During Prohibition, the bar in the Tod House, Youngstown, Ohio, was transformed into a soda fountain. The original bar counter remained in use, ornamented with a mural showing five scenes in the life of Rip Van Winkle. Added was a battery of wooden booths in two rows, back to back thru the center of the room and along one end, as well as a candy counter with a display of house-made sweets. An ambitious menu of ice cream sodas, egg drinks, phosphates, frappes, parfaits, and sundaes, included the shocking-pink American Beauty.

**2 scoops** vanilla ice cream
**3 tablespoons** crushed strawberries
whipped cream, colored with strawberry juice

Into a tulip sundae glass put 1 tablespoon crushed strawberries. Add 2 scoops of vanilla ice cream. Cover with remaining strawberries. Top with "pink" whipped cream.

{ The whip is prepared by adding sweetened and strained strawberry pulp to marshmallow, then whipping lightly. The dainty color that the fruit imparts makes it an attractive decoration. }

*Crushed fresh strawberries are usually sweet enough and heavy enough in consistency for serving when blended with four ounces of simple syrup to a pint basket of fresh strawberries.*

# army-navy sundae

Walter C. Mundt immigrated to America from Germany in 1866, securing a position with confectioners A&J Doescher in Cincinnati, Ohio, where in 1886 he made the wedding cake for 28-year-old William Howard Taft (who would be elected American President 22 years later), and where he supervised the making of ice cream and confections at the 1888 Ohio Centennial Exposition. In 1893 Walter moved his family to Madison, Wisconsin, where he founded Mundt's Candies. True to tradition, the Army-Navy Sundae at Mundt's is served with a "pitcherette" of hot fudge and a French wafer on the side.

**2 scoops** coffee ice cream
**6 ounces** hot fudge sauce
whipped cream
salted almonds, chopped
white chocolate, shaved

Into a tulip sundae glass put 1 ounce hot fudge. Add 2 scoops of coffee ice cream. Top with whipped cream and sprinkle with almonds and white chocolate. Fill a small pitcher with remaining hot fudge sauce and serve on the side.

The "pitcherette" on the side allows you to pour the fudge over the top of the ice cream in one fell swoop or parcel it out over the course of eating your sundae.

From The Bulletin of Pharmacy (1919): "Hot fudge should not be poured over the ice cream until just before placing it in front of the customer. Some stores, indeed, serve the dressing in a separate pitcher, a practice which allows the customer to mix the sundae as he wishes."

# bachelor's kiss

Back in 1908, Angelo Lagomarcino, an immigrant from Northern Italy, founded an eponymous confectionery in Moline, Illinois, operating the business with his wife Luigia and their three children Charlie, Mary, and Tom. In 1912, Angelo paid a traveling salesman $25 for a hot fudge recipe that became the centerpiece of his sundae offerings. Things haven't changed much at Lagomarcino's. You can still slide into one of the original handcrafted mahogany booths for the Batchelor's Kiss, a double-dip sundae that encourages sharing (made with the celebrated hot fudge, of course).

1 **scoop** vanilla ice cream
1 **scoop** chocolate ice cream
3 **ounces** hot fudge sauce
3 **ounces** marshmallow syrup
whipped cream
2 maraschino cherries

Dip scoops of vanilla and chocolate ice creams side by side in an oval dish. Cover the vanilla ice cream with hot fudge, cover the chocolate with marshmallow. Top with whipped cream and garnish with cherries.

From *The Pacific Drug Review* (1920): "Serve a glass of water with every sundae whether requested or not."

*H. L. Mencken, the cranky Baltimore newspaperman, hated the ice cream sundae. He called the "misspelled" dessert a "soda fountain mess," and concluded that it was precisely the strange spelling that was responsible for its popularity.*

# banana skyscraper

While the banana split has maintained no fixed formula over the decades, it has always leaned toward the offbeat. From its 1904 beginnings, the idea of slicing a tropical banana from stem to stern as a base for ice creams and syrups has captured the imaginations of soda fountaineers. In 1936, Penn Pharmacy, near the University of Pennsylvania campus, first served a twice-sliced banana, skillfully placed upright in a sundae goblet, adding a stunning new dimension to the traditional split.

**1 scoop** vanilla ice cream
**1 scoop** chocolate ice cream
**1** banana
**4 ounces** chocolate syrup
**4 ounces** crushed strawberries
whipped cream
maraschino cherry

Into a tall tulip sundae glass put the chocolate syrup. Add the vanilla ice cream. With the peel on, split the banana lengthwise, then cut the split halves again widthwise. Remove peel and place the banana quarters, cut side out, into the glass in an upright position. Add the chocolate ice cream, keeping the banana pieces in place. Cover with the crushed strawberries. Top with whipped cream and garnish with cherry.

*At Edgar's Fountain (Pioneer Drug) in Elk Point, South Dakota,*
*a vertical banana split is called The Rocket.*

# banana split

In 1904, David Strickler became the first to liberate the sundae from the straitjacket of a single scoop of ice cream with one topping. As a 23-year-old clerk at the Tassell Pharmacy in downtown Latrobe, Pennsylvania, he framed three small sundaes with a tropical banana. The Banana Split's popularity was assured when Charles Walgreen made it the feature dish at the fountains of his drugstore chain.

1 **scoop** vanilla ice cream
1 **scoop** chocolate ice cream
1 **scoop** strawberry ice cream
2 **tablespoons** crushed pineapple
3 **ounces** chocolate syrup
2 **tablespoons** crushed strawberries
1 banana
whipped cream
walnuts, chopped
3 maraschino cherries

Into a banana boat, add scoops of vanilla, chocolate, and strawberry ice creams. Cover vanilla ice cream with the crushed pineapple, chocolate ice cream with the chocolate syrup, and strawberry ice cream with the crushed strawberries. With the peel on, split the banana in half lengthwise. Remove peel and place halves on each side of the ice creams, with inside cut facing out. Top with whipped cream, sprinkle with chopped nuts, and garnish with cherries.

*In 1907, a restaurant owner from Wilmington, Ohio, thought he made the first banana split. Unaware of the earlier invention in Latrobe, Ernest Hazard also concocted an ice cream sundae which featured a split banana. Hazard's effort is celebrated annually in Wilmington with a Banana Split Festival.*

# barney google

A long-running American comic strip created in 1919 by Billy De Beck, Barney Google inspired the popular 1923 song, "Barney Google (With the Goo-Goo-Googly Eyes)," and by 1925 a banana based ice cream sundae called "Barney Google" appeared in *The Soda Fountain Dispenser's Formulary*. Who knew that 75 years later Barney Google would inspire the name for an internet search engine?

**1 scoop** vanilla ice cream
**1 scoop** chocolate ice cream
**1/2** banana, peeled, sliced into wheels
**3 tablespoons** crushed pineapple
whipped cream
maraschino cherry

Dip 1 scoop each of vanilla ice cream and chocolate ice cream side by side onto an oval dish. In the center between the two, add the crushed pineapple. Place banana wheels around the ice creams. Top with whipped cream and garnish with cherry.

In hash-house Greek, the abbreviated speech of soda fountain employees, the banana split was either a "houseboat" or a "farmer's lunch."

*From* The American Druggist *and* Pharmaceutical Record *(1916):*
*"The pharmacist usually experiences little difficulty in devising new sundaes and names, the chief difficulty being connected with the improvement of the older popular formulas."*

# baseball triumph

From *How to Run a Store* (1921): "A druggist built up a big soda fountain trade on account of his skill in choosing timely and clever names for sodas and sundaes. On one occasion, the home team won a glorious victory of 8 to 0 over the baseball team of a neighboring town. The druggist had an '8-0 Sundae' on sale ten minutes after the game was over. Although it was an ordinary ice cream with a circle of chocolate fudge, everybody had an '8-0 Sundae.' It was not the ice cream they bought, but the druggist's imagination."

**1 large scoop** vanilla ice cream
**3 tablespoons** crushed strawberries
**1** banana, peeled
whipped cream
chocolate jimmies

Slice banana in half lengthwise, then slice both halves again lengthwise. On a round, flat dish, arrange banana strips as a "baseball diamond." Into the center, spoon the crushed strawberries. Use a spoonful each of whipped cream to form "bases." Dip the "ball" of vanilla ice cream onto the center, and decorate with the chocolate jimmies to mimic the ball's "stitches."

{ According to *Let's Sell Ice Cream* (1947), **adding a split banana to a double hot fudge sundae is called a Touchdown Special, featured at the fountain during football season.** }

*Prohibition greatly increased the popularity of the soda fountain. By the 1920s the improvement of refrigeration allowed these places to serve meals as well, and soda fountains were incorporated into department stores, luncheonettes, grocery stores, tobacco shops, and five-and-dime stores.*

# bee's knees sundae

The term was coined in the 1920s, inspired, some say, by Bee Jackson, the New York dancer credited with introducing the Charleston to Broadway when she appeared at the Silver Slipper nightclub (she went on to become the World Champion Charleston dancer). Throughout the twenties, "bee's knees" joined "cat's pajamas" when referring to the height of excellence, and soda fountains appropriated the slang for a honey-coated sundae.

**2 scoops** vanilla ice cream
**4 ounces** honey, warmed
whipped cream
salted almonds

Warm the honey in a pan of warm water. Into a tulip sundae glass, put 1 ounce of the honey. Add the vanilla ice cream. Cover with remaining honey. Top with whipped cream, sprinkle with the salted almonds.

According to *White's Vest Pocket Sundae Formulary*, **a similar fountain formula was called the Bee Hive Sundae.**

Fran Schumer writes: *"What really distinguishes ice-cream parlors is their atmosphere and therein lies the difference between a sundae that satisfies the palate and one that satisfies the soul."*

# billy sundae

After being a popular outfielder in baseball's National League during the 1880s, Billy Sunday became the most celebrated and influential American evangelist during the first two decades of the 20th century. Sunday was a strong supporter of Prohibition, and his preaching almost certainly played a significant role in the adoption of the Eighteenth Amendment. According to *The Bulletin of Pharmacy* (1919), an ice cream concoction named for the preacher lured patrons out of saloons and into soda fountains.

1 **scoop** vanilla ice cream
1 **scoop** orange sherbet
2 **tablespoons** crushed strawberries
2 **tablespoons** crushed peaches
2 **tablespoons** crushed pineapple
whipped cream
maraschino cherry

Dip scoops of vanilla ice cream and orange sherbet side by side in an oval dish. Cover the vanilla ice cream with the crushed peaches, and cover the orange sherbet with the crushed pineapple. Add crushed strawberries in between. Top with whipped cream and garnish with cherry.

Some say the very name "sundae" was coined by students at Northwestern University after their baseball coach, evangelist Billy Sunday.

From The Retail Druggist (1920): "Under the name of each sundae on the menu or on the wall card, confectioners must list just what is contained in each of the dishes. By doing this, the store gives the customer the chance of ordering just what will please him most."

# birthdae

Confections to mark the anniversary of the day of a person's birth date back as far as the Middle Ages, especially in England, where celebrants received symbolic items such as gold coins, rings and thimbles concealed inside their cakes. Each item was associated with a prediction. For example, a person finding a gold coin in a birthday cake would supposedly become wealthy; a person discovering a thimble would never marry.

**2 scoops** chocolate ice cream
**4 ounces** maple syrup
**2** pretzel sticks
whipped cream
maraschino cherry

Into a tulip sundae glass put 1 ounce of maple syrup. Add 2 scoops of chocolate ice cream. Cover with remaining maple syrup. Top with whipped cream, garnish with cherry, and put a pretzel stick into either side of the sundae.

{ From *The Meyer Druggist* (1921): "Always remember to handle the garnish with prongs or a spoon. Never use your fingers." }

*Serve sundae on a clean paper doily or doily covered plate with a clean, dry, shiny spoon at the side (not in the sundae) next to a napkin and the glass of water. This not only puts the sundae right in the spotlight making it seem exciting and important, but strengthens your customer's feeling that yours is a clean, sanitary soda fountain*

# black and tan sundae

Ice cream parlors in America owe at least some of their popularity to Prohibition. If you couldn't indulge in booze, you could at least eat ice cream. Thus the black and tan sundae may be a suggested alternative to the Irish black and tan, a half and half drink of mixed stout and ale. The 1917 *Bulletin of Pharmacy* provided a formula for the Black and Tan Sundae, along with profitable advice to the pharmacist: "Every fountain patron is a potential buyer for other merchandise."

**1 scoop** chocolate ice cream
**1 scoop** coffee ice cream
**3 ounces** chocolate syrup
**3 ounces** coffee syrup
whipped cream
maraschino cherry

Dip one scoop of coffee ice cream and one scoop of chocolate ice cream side by side on an oval dish. Cover the coffee ice cream with chocolate syrup, and cover the chocolate ice cream with coffee syrup. To with whipped cream and garnish with cherry.

According to *White's Vest Pocket Sundae Formulary*, **a similar fountain formula was called the Broadway Sundae.**

From The Meyer Druggist (*1921*): *"The dispenser need not confine himself to one specialty article; in fact, it is better to have two or three — each one with some individual advantage to attract certain tastes. And in dispensing these specialties, it is important that the quality be fully maintained."*

# black and white sundae

The yin and yang of chocolate and vanilla was never more graciously displayed than in a version of the Black and White Sundae devised by French chef Louis De Gouy, an apprentice of the great Escoffier, and head chef at the Waldorf-Astoria Hotel for 30 years. In his book, *Soda Fountain Luncheonette Drinks and Recipes* (1940), De Gouy explains that sundaes should be served "daintily," and he warns: "Don't fill the sundaes too much, so full that the dressing used runs over the edge."

**1 scoop** vanilla ice cream
**1 scoop** chocolate ice cream
**4** vanilla wafers
**3 ounces** chocolate syrup
**3 ounces** marshmallow syrup
pecans, chopped
walnuts, chopped

Place vanilla wafers on a flat dish so as to form two squares. Dip vanilla ice cream onto one square, chocolate ice cream onto the other. Cover vanilla ice cream with the marshmallow and top with pecans. Cover the chocolate ice cream with chocolate syrup and top with walnuts.

> Outside of the venerable Waldorf, the classic sundae
> is sometimes called a Spotted Dog.

*When a plain sundae is topped with a ladle of whipped cream and decorated with a cherry it is called a "French Sundae." It was customary for fountains to charge an extra five cents for these sundaes; the amount of whipped cream was generous and not to be confused with the little dab sometimes used for decoration only.*

# black night sundae

The Sealtest brand was originally a franchise, with local dairies purchasing rights to the trademark in their market areas. In the 1950s, Sealtest brand milk and ice cream products sponsored national network broadcasting, including the *Sealtest Big Top* on CBS-TV. The circus-theme show featured Ed McMahon (later on *Tonight Show* fame) as the clown, actor Jack Sterling as the ringmaster, and Dan Luri as the Sealtest bodybuilder. National magazine ads for Sealtest promoted "The Best Ice Cream in a Month of Sundaes," including an all-chocolate sundae for the 30th day.

**2 scoops** chocolate ice cream
**4 ounces chocolate syrup**
walnuts, chopped

Into a tulip sundae glass put 1 ounce chocolate syrup. Add 2 scoops chocolate ice cream. Cover with remaining chocolate syrup and sprinkle walnuts over the top.

According to *White's Vest Pocket Sundae Formulary*, **similar fountain formulas might have been called Chocolate Noodle or Chocolate Dope.**

*"Drop a bucket of mud with a black bottom!" That's how a waiter barked an order to a soda jerk for a double chocolate sundae. Depending on the fountain, the dish might also have been called a Black-Out Sundae or a Black Diamond Sundae.*

# bone dry sundae

According to *The New Castle News*, a Pennsylvania newspaper, in 1916: "The sundae consists of ice cream smothered in everything except young onions. Owing to the Prohibition wave, thousands of skillful bartenders have been thrown out of employment, but most of them have since been hired to manufacture the ice cream sundae in long wriggling relays. Every few days some former barkeeper will bring out a new sundae which is harder to cook than a welsh rarebit in a hay cooker." Without a sauce or syrup, the Bone Dry Sundae was a deviation from conventional wisdom.

**1 scoop** vanilla ice cream
**1 scoop** chocolate ice cream
**2 tablespoons** shredded coconut
whipped cream
walnuts, chopped
maraschino cherry

Dip scoops of vanilla and chocolate ice creams side by side on an oval dish. In the center between the two, add the shredded coconut. Top with whipped cream, sprinkle with chopped walnuts, and garnish with cherry.

When a flat plate or platter is used, then level off the ice cream scoop portion so that it will sit firmly on the dish.

*Interest in coconuts produced hardly a nod until 1895 when Franklin Baker, a Philadelphia flour miller, received a ship load of coconuts in payment of a debt from a Cuban businessman. After unsuccessful attempts to sell the cargo before they spoiled, he made a decision that put coconuts into the hands of commercial confectioners and soda fountains. He set up a factory for shredding and drying the coconut meat.*

# boston sundae

It's a tricky business, but the folks at Purity Ice Cream have mastered the art of floating a sundae on top of a milkshake, the evolution of a Boston Ice Cream Soda. The "Boston" is the magnum opus of sundaes served at this legendary Ithaca, New York, ice cream parlor. Purity dates back to 1936 when German immigrant Leo Guentert began making local, small-batch ice creams on his own after graduating from Cornell, and the tradition continues under Bruce and Heather Lane. Properly served with both a long spoon and "sissy sticks" (two straws).

**2 scoops** chocolate ice cream
**5 ounces** chocolate syrup
**1/2 cup** of milk
**1 scoop** vanilla ice cream
whipped cream
maraschino cherry

In blender combine 2 scoops of chocolate ice cream, 3 ounces of chocolate syrup, and 1/2 cup of milk. Blend until smooth. Pour into tall goblet. Float 1 scoop of vanilla ice cream at the top of the milkshake. Cover with remaining chocolate syrup. Top with whipped cream and garnish with cherry .

According to *The Dispenser's Formulary*, **a similar fountain formula was called the Pretty Mickey.**

*At some fountains this formula was called a "Mondae," served in tall, narrow gobetss similar to soda glasses, with tops that opened wide like sundae tulips. The bottom was filled with the milkshake, while the top accommodated a scoop of ice cream with syrup, whipped cream and cherry.*

# boy scout

Since their inception in 1910, the Boy Scouts of America have prepared many famous men for adulthood and even public service. The organization has followed Robert Baden-Powell's dream of transforming the youth of the world, providing them with adult companionship, tests of skill and endurance, and middle-class Protestant values emphasizing hard work, thrift, honesty, reliability, and leadership.

**4 ounces** marshmallow syrup
**2 scoops** vanilla ice cream
**1 tablespoon** crushed maraschino cherries
**1 tablespoon** blueberries

Into a tulip sundae glass put 1 ounce marshmallow syrup. Add 2 scoops of vanilla ice cream. Cover with remaining marshmallow. Spoon cherries on one side of the glass, blueberries on the opposite side, leaving a white stripe down the middle.

{ From *The Bulletin of Pharmacy* (1917), on consistency: "The true science of dispensing lies in always having your dishes come out the same." }

*The Washington House Hotel in Two Rivers, Wisconsin, filled with relics from the old Ed Berner's soda fountain, creates a version of this World War II formula called the Washington House Sundae*

# brown derby

Who put the hole in the doughnut? It was a sea captain from Rockport, Maine, who poked out the centers of his wife's fried cakes so he could slip them over the spokes of his ship's wheel, allowing him to nibble while keeping an even keel. The hole provides a perfect vehicle for "dunking," and in soda fountain slang, an order for doughnuts and coffee order came out "sinkers and suds." When a chocolate doughnut becomes a base for chocolate ice cream with chocolate syrup, it's called a Brown Derby. (At the Dairy Dome in Stoneham, Massachusetts, freshly fried dough becomes the base for vanilla ice cream with caramel, it's a Fried Dough Sundae).

> **1 scoop** chocolate ice cream
> **4 ounces** chocolate syrup
> **1** doughnut
> whipped cream
> maraschino cherry

Place doughnut at the center of a flat dish. Dip chocolate ice cream on top of the doughnut. Cover with chocolate syrup. Top with whipped cream and garnish with cherry.

{ Chocolate topping for sundaes and specials should be twice
as heavy as chocolate syrup used in sodas. }

*Opened in 1929, the Brown Derby was a landmark restaurant in Los Angeles, California frequented by celebrities during the Golden Age of Hollywood, the shape of the building inspired by Al Smith's derby hat.*

# brownie bottom sundae

History has it that the brownie was invented in Chicago by the chef of the Palmer House Hotel during the 1893 Columbian Exposition. Socialite Bertha Palmer, it seems, requested a dessert for ladies attending the fair, insisting that it be smaller than a piece of cake, and easily eaten from boxed lunches. The original Palmer House recipe for rich, "gooey" brownies was later popularized as the base for a sundae by Hot Shoppe restaurants, established in Washington D.C. in 1927 by J. Willard Marriott, best known for founding the Marriott Corporation.

**1** brownie, cut into 4" x 4" square
**1 scoop** vanilla ice cream
**4 ounces** hot fudge
whipped cream
maraschino cherry

Place brownie on a flat dish. Add 1 scoop of vanilla ice cream. Cover with hot fudge. Top with whipped cream and garnish with cherry.

From *Drug Topics* (1920): "The soda fountain is the most valuable, most useful, most profitable, and altogether most beneficial business building feature assimilated by the drugstore in a generation."

*At legendary Ghirardelli's in San Francisco, a chocolate chip cookie served under a layer of vanilla ice cream and hot fudge is called the Cookie Bottom Sundae; at Ella's Deli in Madison, Wisconsin, a slice of pound cake becomes the base of the Grilled Pound Cake Sundae.*

# budget sundae

Frank Winfield Woolworth opened five-and-dime stores that became fixtures in American downtowns during the first half of the 20th century. Woolworth made his customers feel "rich" in hard times, and generated immense customer loyalty with five and ten cent treats at the requisite soda fountain in every store. Like a home run in baseball, the chocolate sundae always got the lion's share of attention at the Woolworth's fountain. At a price of one thin dime, Woolworth dubbed his single-scoop special a "Budget Sundae."

**1 scoop** vanilla ice cream
**3 ounces** chocolate syrup
whipped cream
maraschino cherry

Into a tulip sundae glass put 1 ounce chocolate syrup. Add 1 scoop vanilla ice cream. Cover with remaining chocolate syrup. Top with whipped cream and garnish with cherry.

Legendary confectioner Milton Snavely Hershey once said:
"Caramels are only a fad. Chocolate is a permanent thing."

From The International Confectioner (1919): "The average fountain is simply a list of drinks and sundaes, many of the names being utterly meaningless to the average customer, who, having read a lot of names, comes to the conclusion that he or she will play safe and order a chocolate sundae. A menu should be more than a list, and an unintelligible one at that."

# buffalo sundae

Claude D. Smith came to Grand Junction, Colorado, in 1900, at age twenty-one. Already a certified pharmacist, young Smith and a partner bought the Adams Drug Store, on the southwest corner of 5th and Main. Smith was able to buy out his partner in two-and one- half years, with success eventually allowing him to purchase six more drug stores, located in Fruita, Grand Junction, Palisade, Debeque, and in Grand Valley (modern-day Parachute). Smith's soda fountains served all the regular fountain drinks, including phosphates, and ice cream treats included the specialty "Walnut and Buffalo Sundae, both rich and smooth."

**2 scoops** vanilla ice cream
**4 ounces** chocolate syrup
walnuts, chopped
whipped cream
maraschino cherry

Place brownie on a flat dish. Add 1 scoop of vanilla ice cream. Cover with hot fudge. Top with whipped cream and garnish with cherry.

Thomas and Charles Stoddart opened Stoddart Brothers Drug Store at 84 East Seneca Street in Buffalo, New York, the first location in the city to install a soda fountain.

Northwestern Druggist magazine (1913) described another version of the Buffalo Sundae as "chocolate ice cream, marshmallow slices and cherries."

# c.m.p. sundae

Marshmallow became a popular sundae topping during World War II because most chocolate was being used for the Armed Forces, and while whole eggs were rationed, powdered egg whites were not. After the war, fountain customers were delighted to have their chocolate syrup back, but since they had developed a taste for marshmallow, a combination of both sauces began to appear. Originating in the coal region towns of Pennsylvania, the C.M.P. Sundae, adding the crunch of peanuts, became the popular favorite in local ice cream parlors.

**2 scoops** vanilla ice cream
**3 ounces** chocolate syrup
**3 ounces** marshmallow syrup
**1/3 cup** salted peanuts, whole

Dip 2 scoops of vanilla ice cream side by side on an oval dish. Cover one scoop of ice cream with the chocolate syrup, and cover the other with the marshmallow. Layer the top with peanuts.

From *The Pacific Drug Review* (1920): "Serve a paper napkin (7" x 14"), folded once over, with all sundaes, placing the napkin under the dish or glass."

From American Druggist Magazine (1906): "The introduction of the sundae is credited to the soda fountain trade as it goes over the counter and it seems to be very much in favor on the part of the seller."

# canadian special

In 1917, *Canadian Druggist* magazine featured the recipe for a sundae assembled on a confection with its own history. In 18th century Europe, fruitcakes were made using nuts from the harvest for good luck in the following year. The cake was then saved and eaten before the harvest of the next year. By the 19th century, the fruitcake was popular at Victorian Teas in England. Fruitcake is both an American and Canadian Christmas tradition.

**1 scoop** strawberry ice cream
**1 slice** fruit cake
**3 ounces** marshmallow syrup
whipped cream
pecans, chopped
maraschino cherry

Place fruitcake on a flat dish. Add 1 scoop of strawberry ice cream. Cover with marshmallow. Top with whipped cream, sprinkle with pecans, and garnish with cherry.

"Chopped and iced fruits, commonly known as fruit cocktails," according to *Canadian Druggist*, "always find favor with children, and may be substituted for the richer ice cream sundaes."

*Mail-order fruitcakes in America began in 1913. With its access to cheap nuts, Southern bakeries included more nuts in their recipes, and by 1935, the expression "nutty as a fruitcake" became part of American lexicon.*

# cashew delight sundae

According to a 1920 issue of *The Bulletin of Pharmacy*, "Druggists who keep accurate cost records have realized that but little profit results from serving a sundae for ten cents. So accustomed has the public become to obtaining a fancy sundae in exchange for a thin dime that unless something special is offered, a higher price is not easy to obtain. This 'something special' at many fountains takes the form of dressings that contain nut meats." This advice is taken to heart at the venerable Tom's Ice Cream Bowl in Zanesville, Ohio, where an assortment of nuts is freshly-roasted daily.

**2 scoops** vanilla ice cream
**4 ounces** hot fudge
**1/2 cup** salted cashews, whole
whipped cream
maraschino cherry

Into a tulip sundae glass put 1 ounce hot fudge. Add 2 scoops vanilla ice cream. Cover with remaining hot fudge and cashews. Top with whipped cream and garnish with cherry.

{ According to Philip G. Keeney of Penn State's Department of Dairy Science: "Roasted nuts are less likely to absorb moisture than untreated nuts." }

*Chiya Fujino writes: "Nuts topping a sundae introduce a crunch, crunch, crunch to the sweet melody, like a pair of castanets."*

# chaplin charlie

A story is told that a screenwriter once asked Charlie Chaplin "How, can I make a fat lady, walking down Fifth Avenue, slip on a banana peel and get a laugh? Do I show first the banana peel, then the fat lady approaching, then she slips? Or do I show the fat lady first, then the banana peel, and THEN she slips?" "Neither," said Chaplin. "You show the fat lady approaching; then you show the banana peel; then you show the fat lady and the banana peel together; then she steps OVER the banana peel and disappears down a manhole." At 1920s fountains, a backwards-named version of a banana sundae was sure to follow.

**1** banana, peeled
**1 scoop** strawberry ice cream
**4 ounces** chocolate syrup
whipped cream
salted peanuts, crushed

Dip 1 scoop of strawberry ice cream onto the center of a flat dish. Cover with chocolate syrup. Split the banana in half widthwise, and place each half upright at either side of the ice cream. Top each upright banana with whipped cream and sprinkle crushed peanuts over all.

From *Let's Sell Ice Cream* (1947): "Select a fully-ripe medium sized banana. Split it in half lengthwise, with the peel on."

From The Bulletin of Pharmacy (1917): "The pharmacist, with increasingly less time devoted to compounding drugs, supplemented his income by adding various elements to the drugstore. One of the most important and romanticized was the soda fountain, where the pharmacist dispensed ice cream sodas and sundaes."

# chicago sundae

In 1935, Gus Poulos began serving homemade ice cream at a two table stand called Homer's in Chicago's North Shore suburb of Wilmette. His ice cream was richer than any other in that era, anywhere in Chicago. From its humble beginnings, Homer's has grown to become the quintessential ice cream parlor, with brick walls, festive red-and-white interior, and old-fashioned ball lights. Legend has it that, after serving his term in Alcatraz in 1939, Al Capone bought a lakefront house not far from Homer's. The head of the "Chicago Outfit" visited often for an ice cream treat.

**2 scoops** vanilla ice cream
**3 tablespoons** crushed pineapple
whipped cream
maraschino cherry

Into a tulip sundae glass put 1 tablespoon crushed pineapple. Add 2 scoops of vanilla ice cream. Cover with remaining pineapple. Top with whipped cream and garnish with cherry.

According to *White's Vest Pocket Sundae Formulary*, **a similar fountain formula was called the Sunshine Sundae.**

*During the 1920s, servers at Chicago fountains drew a connection between the pineapple topping and the slang term "pineapple," for grenade used by Chicago gangsters, because of the similar shape and the criss-cross pattern common to both.*

# chop suey double sundae

Beginning in the mid-19th century, Chinese immigrants settled their own Chinatowns within major United States cities, where they opened chow chow lunchrooms. At first these small, cramped eateries catered to their own people, then expanded their menus to attract curious Americans who dared cross into those mysterious cities- within-cities. Native cuisine got mixed up with American traditions, producing this fountain concoction listed in *The National Soda Fountain Guide* (1913).

**2 scoops** vanilla ice cream
**1 tablespoon** raisins
**1 tablespoon** dates, chopped
**1 tablespoon** figs, chopped
**4 ounces** maple syrup
shredded coconut
maraschino cherry

Chop raisins, dates, and figs, and mix together with the maple syrup. Dip scoops of ice cream side by side in an oval dish. Ladle the chop suey mix between the scoops and sprinkle shredded coconut over the top. Garnish with cherry.

{ Chop Suey, a Chinese-American dish prepared from "leftovers," was first offered in the 1920s as an ice cream sundae (for 20 cents) at the Chocolate Garden, a dessert parlor in Venice, California. }

*Soda fountain waitstaff and kitchen workers communicated orders in colorful, quirky "calls." If you were in one of these places between 1925 and 1945, you might have overheard a sundae called a "bellyache."*

# christmas special

The maraschino cherry is grown in the northwestern United States, pitted, and then processed. It has a bright color added to make it appear festive. The common colors are red and green. To keep the fruit longer, it is coated in a fructose slur which gives it a candied covering. Both colors were used in this 1930s "Holiday" formula promoted by Pennant Brand of Portland, Oregon, makers of sundae toppings and soda fountain syrups.

**1 scoop** vanilla ice cream
**1 scoop** strawberry ice cream
**3 tablespoons** crushed strawberries
whipped cream
pecans, chopped
**3** maraschino cherries (red)
**3** maraschino cherries (green**)**

Into a tulip sundae glass put 1 tablespoon of crushed strawberries. Add scoop of vanilla ice cream, then scoop of strawberry ice cream. Cover with remaining crushed strawberries. Top with whipped cream, sprinkle with walnuts, and garnish with red and green cherries.

{ Red and green, the traditional colors of Christmas, originated with holly (red) and pine tree branches (green) usedin the pagan celebration of winter solstice or "Yule." }

*From* The Meyer Druggist *(1921): "Granting a neat fountain, the druggist should have a responsible attendant. An inexperienced and slovenly attendant is always a source of dissatisfaction to customers and a detriment to the increase of the store's general business. Get the best attendant you can afford."*

# co-ed sundae

Doumar's of Norfolk is marked by a sign with two big ice cream cones on either side, a reminder that Abe Doumar, the founder, invented the ice cream cone. You can still get your ice cream served in a freshly-made waffle cone, but the Co-ed Sundae (called "Pride of the House") has long enjoyed canonical status at Doumar's.

**2 scoops** vanilla ice cream
**2 ounces** chocolate syrup
**2 ounces** marshmallow syrup
**1** banana
whipped cream
walnuts, chopped
maraschino cherry

Dip scoops of vanilla and chocolate ice creams side by side on a banana split dish. Cover one scoop of ice cream with chocolate syrup, the other scoop with marshmallow. With the peel on, split the banana lengthwise. Remove peel and place halves on either side of the ice cream. Top with whipped cream, sprinkle with walnuts, and garnish with cherry.

"There are several ways of making banana splits," according to the trade publication, *What Every Ice Cream Dealer Should Know* (1914), "and many of the dealers use several of the most convenient fruits which they have on hand."

*Teens of the 20s invented dating. It was a more flexible way of meeting and seeing each other that was not as supervised as it had been in the past. Previously, boys had to be courting a girl, they had to be committed, and girls had to be engaged to them in order to go out with them.*

# coffee "roon"

In 1936, Professor Harold W. Bentley of Columbia University document-
ed the peculiarly American phenomenon of "camouflaged soda fountain
language" in *Linguistic Concoctions of the Soda Jerkers*. A sign of the times,
the soda jerker's effectiveness was judged in part on the basis of his ability to show off the fountain by the witty use of such lingo as "coff" for coffee ice cream, the principal ingredient in a popular "dry" sundae.

**2 scoops** coffee ice cream
**2 tablespoons** macaroon crumbs
whipped cream
pineapple cube

Into a tulip sundae glass add 2 scoops of coffee ice cream. Cover
with the macaroon crumbs. Top with whipped cream and garnish
with pineapple cube.

As an alternative, this sundae can be made using maple
or chocolate ice cream. Change name according
to the flavor of ice cream used.

From The Meyer Druggist (1921): "The soda fountain clerk who has the ability to attract
people to his fountain because they prefer to come to him for service rather than
to go to some other place where they would receive just as much in quantity,
has scored a victory that is worth much in the business world."

# coney island sundae

No other sundae name was represented by as many different formulas. The 1909 *Dispenser Soda Water Guide* described a Coney Island Sundae as: "ice cream with red cherry syrup, and whipped cream topped with orange syrup and a maraschino cherry." A year later, *The Bulletin of Pharmacy* version was: "orange sherbet in the shape of a cigar and some vanilla ice cream in the same shape; lay them together in a saucer, then top with a ladle of chopped pineapple, a ladle of whipped cream, and a cherry." Philadelphia's Franklin Fountain offers a contemporary interpretation.

**2 scoops** chocolate ice cream
**4 ounces** marshmallow syrup
**1 tablespoon** orange marmalade
whipped cream
candied orange peel

Into a tulip sundae glass put 1 ounce marshmallow. Add 2 scoops of chocolate ice cream. Cover with remaining marshmallow. Spoon orange marmalade onto the top, and add whipped cream. Garnish with candied orange peel.

> Proprietors Eric and Ryan Berley named their "ice cream saloon" after Philadelphia's own Benjamin Franklin, who had operated his first business in the same neighborhood.

*From* American Druggist and Pharmaceutical Record *(1906): "Granting a neat, fountain, the druggist should have a responsible attendant. An Inexperienced and slovenly attendant Is always a source of dissatisfaction to customers and a detriment to the Increase of the store's general business."*

# cracker jill

Immortalized in the classic song, "Take Me Out to the Ball Game," Cracker Jack has earned a place in the hearts and stomachs of Americans since it was introduced at the World's Fair in Chicago in 1893. The name came along three years later when, according to legend, a salesman, upon tasting the treat for the first time, proclaimed, "That's a Cracker Jack!" The name was patented and a brand was born. When Cracker Jack was added to a chocolate sundae, it was named for the other half of the nursery rhyme twosome.

**2 scoops** vanilla ice cream
**4 ounces** chocolate syrup
**3 tablespoons** Cracker Jack
whipped cream
maraschino cherry

Into a tulip sundae glass put 1 ounce chocolate syrup. Add 1 tablespoon Cracker Jack, then the 2 scoops of vanilla ice cream. Cover with remaining chocolate syrup, then add remaining Cracker Jack. Top with whipped cream and garnish with cherry.

Cracker Jack was not the only "spoon novelty" used at the fountain. Rice Krispies were added to marshmallow topping in a Krispy Marshmallow Sundae.

In 1910, coupons were included in Cracker Jack boxes which could be redeemed for prizes. It wasn't until 1912 that children's prizes (miniature books, magnifying glasses, tiny pitchers, beans, metal trains, etc.) were place in the boxes. The company slogan was "a prize-in-every-package.

# david harum

Half the fun of early soda fountain sundaes was each new name they come up with for a new formula. From one of the early 20th century's best-selling novels (whose legacy is the colloquial use of the term "horse trading"), a fountain concoction was named for small town banker and horse trader, David Harum. The character's version of the Golden Rule ("Do unto the other feller the way he'd like to do unto you, and do it first") came into popular use as an approbatory term for what others would deem ethically dubious business practices.

**2 scoops** vanilla ice cream
**2 tablespoons** crushed strawberries
**2 tablespoons** crushed pineapple
whipped cream
maraschino cherry

Into the bottom of a long narrow parfait glass ladle 1 tablespoon crushed strawberries. Add 1 scoop of vanilla ice cream into the glass. Cover with 1 tablespoon crushed pineapple. Add a second scoop of the ice cream into the glass and top with remaining strawberries and pineapple. Top with whipped cream and garnish with cherry.

From *The Pacific Drug Review* (1920): "A good original sundae name combined with a good original concoction is a strong combination."

*The artistic features of the menu depend principally upon the class of trade to which you are catering. What is a pleasing and appropriate menu for a fountain appealing to a fashionable woman's trade would be an abomination for the fountain in a business section. There ought to be a great deal of difference in a menu that is used by college student patrons and one placed before the trade of a suburban store.*

# don't care sundae

Schwab's Drugstore, on Sunset Boulevard in Hollywood, California was once the meeting place of movie actors and dealmakers. During its lifespan, from the 1930s through the 1950s, insiders referred to Schwab's as "headquarters." Typical of many drug stores in that period, the store had a counter serving ice cream dishes and light meals. Hollywood legend holds that Lana Turner was discovered at Schwab's fountain, although the event actually occurred at a malt shop about a mile away.

**2 scoops** coffee ice cream
**4 ounces** chocolate syrup
whipped cream
maraschino cherry

Into a tulip sundae glass put 1 ounce chocolate syrup. Add 2 scoops of coffee ice cream. Cover with remaining chocolate syrup. Top with whipped cream and garnish with cherry.

Harold Arlen wrote "Over the Rainbow" while sitting in his car in front of Schwab's Drugstore.

During Prohibition, a healthy splash of hard liquor found its way into soda water glasses at some fountains, and the expression, "Don't Care" became the term for these special mixtures when a customer was thirsting for a stimulant.

# double feature sundae

In the mid-1930s, a visit to the movie theater was welcome relief from the hard times of the day. While Nick and Nora sipped martinis in *The Thin Man*, and Mickey and Judy shared an ice cream soda in *Life Begins for Andy Hardy*, Laurel and Hardy ordered a banana split in *Man 'O War*, and Fred treated Ginger to an ice cream sundae in *The Fleet's In*. Ten-cent movies like ten-cent sundaes were something of an antidote to the great drought of the period.

**1 scoop** vanilla ice cream
**1 scoop** chocolate ice cream
**3 ounces** chocolate syrup
**3 ounces** marshmallow syrup
whipped cream
walnuts, chopped
maraschino cherry

Dip scoop of vanilla ice cream and scoop of chocolate ice cream side by side in an oval dish. Cover the vanilla ice cream with chocolate syrup, cover the chocolate ice cream with marshmallow. Top with whipped cream, sprinkle with walnuts, and garnish with cherries.

In the classic W. C. Fields comedy, *Never Give a Sucker an Even Break*, a scene that was supposed to take place in a saloon was changed to a soda fountain by the Motion Picture Production Code.

In *Flying Down to Rio*, *Fred Astaire plays Fred Ayers and Ginger Rogers plays Honey Hale: "Suppose we do a number with musical swords, and we can end up cutting Honey in half?" asks Fred. "I'd much rather split a banana split three ways," replies Honey.*

# dunce cap sundae

The reference to a "dunce cap" first appeared in the 1840 novel, *The Old Curiosity Shop* by Charles Dickens. The conical cap was used as a method of punishment through public humiliation in school classrooms. Students who were slow, lazy, or considered to be stupid were forced to sit in the corner of the classroom with a dunce cap. It was inevitable that an aspiring sundae maker would notice the resemblance between the edible cone for serving ice cream and the amusing headgear.

**2 scoops** vanilla ice cream
**2 tablespoons** crushed strawberries
**2 tablespoons** crushed pineapple
salted peanuts, crushed
whipped cream
**1** sugar cone

Into a tulip sundae glass put 1/2 tablespoon crushed strawberries and 1/2 tablespoon crushed pineapple. Add 2 scoops of vanilla ice cream. Cover with remaining strawberries and pineapple. Sprinkle peanuts over the top. Fill the sugar cone with whipped cream, invert and place on top.

The ice cream cone was invented in St. Louis, Missouri in 1904 at the Louisiana Purchase Exposition, a crisp pastry cooked in a hot waffle-patterned press coming to the aid of a neighboring ice cream vendor who had run out of dishes.

*Syrian immigrant Abe Doumar developed a four-iron machine that rolled his native zalabia into cones. In 1905 he opened ice cream stands at Coney Island and "Little Coney Island" in North Bergen, New Jersey, before settling in Norfolk, Virginia, where Doumar's has become something of a local legend.*

# dusty miller sundae

Early drugstore soda fountains promoted the combination of ice cream and malted milk as a complete meal, citing its use as a provision for the era's North Pole and South Pole expeditions by Robert Peary, Roald Amundsen, and Robert Falcon Scott. Before long, Horlick's, the original manufacturer of malted milk, was being widely imitated by rivals including Carnation and Borden's. In soda fountain slang, malted milk was often called "hops," and the Dusty Road Sundae spawned a hops-topped cousin called Dusty Miller.

**2 scoops** vanilla ice cream
**3 ounces** chocolate syrup
**2 ounces** marshmallow
**1 tablespoon + 1/2 teaspoon** malted milk powder
whipped cream

Into a tulip sundae glass put 1 ounce of the chocolate syrup. Add the vanilla ice cream. Cover with remaining chocolate syrup, then the marshmallow. Top with 1 tablespoon of malted milk powder, then whipped cream. Dust with 1/2 teaspoon of malted milk powder.

> "Malt shops" owe their very name to the Horlick brothers, two British men who started out to make a malted milk drink for infants.

*In 1922, Stephen Poplawski had the idea of putting a rotating blade at the bottom of a container. He invented the blender for the specific use of allowing milkshakes and malts to be made easily at home*

# dusty road sundae

Originally manufactured in the 1870s by William and James Horlick as an infant food, malted milk became better known as the toasty flavoring in double-rich chocolate malted milkshakes offered at Walgreens drugstore lunch counters, beginning with the invention of the electric blender in 1922. As malts became universally popular soda fountain drinks, it wasn't long before malted milk powder was employed as a "dusty" topping for the chocolate sundae.

**2 scoops** coffee ice cream
**4 ounces** chocolate syrup
**1 tablespoon + 1/2 teaspoon** malted milk powder
whipped cream

Into a tulip sundae glass put 1 ounce of the chocolate syrup. Add the coffee ice cream. Cover with remaining chocolate syrup. Top with 1 tablespoon of malted milk powder, then whipped cream. Dust with 1/2 teaspoon of malted milk powder.

According to the 1938 Borden's Formulary for Soda Fountain Operators, a similar fountain formula was called the Jersey Special.

*A twelve-to-the-quart scoop is used for plain ice cream and sundaes, and a sixteen-to-the-quart scoop for ice cream sodas and banana royals. Sometimes a twenty-to-the-quart scoop is used for banana splits and other fancy fruit specialties.*

# early bird sundae

From *The Meyer Druggist* (1921): "You can just as well have a new fountain ready for operation the first warm day of spring as to miss a week or two while a competitor is getting people into the habit of coming his way. It is the 'early bird' that catches the early soda water trade, and the one who gets the early trade and gets customers started his way at the opening of the season has the advantage over him who opens later."

**1 scoop** vanilla ice cream
**1 scoop** chocolate ice cream
**4 ounces** hot butterscotch
whipped cream
grape nuts, crushed
maraschino cherry

Into a tulip sundae glass put 1 ounce of butterscotch. Add scoop of vanilla ice cream, then scoop of chocolate ice cream. Cover with remaining butterscotch. Top with whipped cream, sprinkle with grape nuts, and garnish with cherry.

{ "Don'ts" for the soda fountain man from *Rigby's Reliable Candy Teacher* (1921) include: "Don't fail to wear a white coat and apron and be sure these are clean." }

From Let's Sell Ice Cream *(1947)*: "Serve the sundae on a clean paper doily or doily-covered plate with a clean, shiny spoon at the side (not in the sundae) next to a napkin and a glass of water — and with a smile from you."

# flood of '36 sundae

On March 16, 1936, warmer-than-normal temperatures led to the melting of snow and ice into the Allegheny and Monongahela rivers, threatening the city of Pittsburgh. By the next day, the waters reached flood stage, and heavy rains overnight caused the waters to rise quickly, peaking at 46 feet, and up to the tin ceiling at Klavon's Pharmacy. Ever since, Klavon's has commemorated its survival of the "Great St. Patrick's Day Flood" with a sundae at the fountain.

**2 scoops** vanilla ice cream
**4 ounces** ho t fudge
**1 tablespoon** crushed Oreos
whipped cream
chocolate jimmies

Into a tulip sundae glass put 1 ounce hot fudge. Add 2 scoops of vanilla ice cream. Cover with remaining hot fudge and sprinkle with crushed Oreos. Top with whipped cream and sprinkle with chocolate jimmies.

Klavon's serves each sundae with a pretzel ring over the tall spoon, the salt providing harmonious counterpoint to the sweet.

From The Retail Druggist (1920): "It is a pleasure to watch the rapid, skilful motions of a trained dispenser as he takes the orders and quickly and neatly prepares them without any unnecessary juggling. When a dispenser works with perfect ease it impresses the people with the idea that he knows his business and that the sundaes must be good."

# floradora sundae

The name comes from one of the first successful Broadway musicals of the 20th century, its success attributed to a sextet of chorines, called "the English Girls" in the score, but popularly dubbed the "Florodora Girls." The six roles were filled by identically-sized women, all five-feet-four-inches tall, and all weighing exactly one hundred and thirty pounds. Young male admirers persuaded many to leave the show to marry them, and soda fountains glorified them with a Floradora Sundae.

**1 tablespoon** chopped cherries
**2 scoops** vanilla ice cream
**2 tablespoons** crushed pineapple
whipped cream
maraschino cherry

Into a tulip sundae glass put 1 tablespoon chopped cherries. Add 2 scoops of vanilla ice cream. Cover with 2 tablespoons of crushed pineapple. Top with whipped cream and garnish with cherry.

> The musical film, *Florodora Girl*, made in 1930, starred Marion Davies as a chorus girl playing one of the English girls in the original Broadway production of Florodora.

*Schrafft's was a New York institution, a lunchroom with candy and ice cream that once seemed indispensable, then vanished without a trace. Its Broadway Sundae, intended for "ladies who lunch," consisted of one small scoop of chocolate, served in a shallow glass dish with chocolate sauce, seven fine toasted almonds.*

# fountaineer special

J. Hungerford Smith graduated from the University of Michigan in 1877 with a degree of Pharmaceutical Chemist. In 1880 he began experimenting with fruit syrups dispensed from soda fountains. Moving to Rochester, New York, in 1890, he organized the J. Hungerford Smith Company and began the manufacture of "True Fruit" syrups, which became the industry standard. The Fountaineer Special was devised by the J. Hungerford Smith Testing and Research Laboratory.

**1 scoop** vanilla ice cream
**1 scoop** chocolate ice cream
**3 ounces chocolate syrup**
**2 tablespoons** crushed pineapple
whipped cream
maraschino cherry

Dip one scoop of vanilla ice cream and one scoop of chocolate ice cream side by side on an oval dish. Cover the vanilla ice cream with chocolate syrup, and cover the chocolate ice cream with crushed pineapple. Top with whipped cream and garnish with cherry.

From the J. Hungerford Smith *Fountain Formula Book*: "A dash of whipped cream, a garnish of fruit, a contrast of color, transforms an ordinary sundae or frappé into a palate-tempting island of desire."

In 1930, Sherman Kelly of Toledo, Ohio, invented the Zeroll, a non-mechanical, one-handed ice cream scoop. Its thick handle is comfortable for large and small hands, and its self-defrosting liquid (which responds to heat from the user's hand) contributes to perfect release, leaving only traces of melted cream inside the scoop.

# george washington sundae

Did George Washington chop down a cherry tree and tell his father the truth? The first President's connection to cherry trees and confections, it seems, lies on somewhat shaky ground. Historians claim that author Parson Mason Weems added the cherry tree story to an early biography in order to liven up Washington's somewhat solemn history and, of course, to increase book sales. Undaunted by the facts, an early soda fountain sundae formula was as American as, well, cherry pie.

**1 scoop** vanilla ice cream
**6** maraschino cherries, stems removed
whipped cream
salted almonds, crushed

Into a tulip sundae glass add 1 scoop of vanilla ice cream. Place maraschino cherries in a ring around the edge. Top with whipped cream and sprinkle with almonds.

If you add crushed pineapple to the formula, it becomes a Merry Widow Sundae.

*Elizabeth "Betsy" Hamilton, wife of Alexander Hamilton first served ice cream to George Washington in 1789. Afterwards, it was often served at the Presidential Thursday dinners.*

# gold rush sundae

Earle Swensen, the son of a Norwegian brick mason, started making ice cream on a Navy troop ship in the South Pacific during World War II. He said the sailors didn't care what flavor he made – they just wanted something cold in the hot climate. Back in San Francisco, he opened an ice cream store on Hyde and Union Streets in 1948. He began franchising in the 1960s with the idea that each owner could operate his own store, and by 1976 he was grossing over $20 million a year. He sold the chain in the early 1980s but kept the original store, where the Gold Rush Sundae is still being scooped.

**1 scoop** chocolate
**1 scoop** coffee ice cream
**3 ounces** hot butterscotch
**3 ounces** hot fudge
whipped cream
salted almonds, crushed

Dip scoops of chocolate and coffee ice creams side by side in an oval dish. Cover the chocolate with the hot fudge, and cover the coffee ice cream with the butterscotch. Top with whipped cream and sprinkle almonds over the top.

Swensen's sundae was named in honor of the early prospectors who traveled to California in search of the American Dream. It was one of the greatest adventures the world had ever seen.

*In 1906, Los Angeles boasted the largest soda fountain in the world, Fothgale's, featuring a black marble counter 72 feet long and columns of onyx and silver supporting a canopy in Mission style.*

# grand central sundae

Soon after Grand Central Terminal officially opened on February 2, 1913, it became the busiest train station in the country. In 1947, more than 65 million people, the equivalent of 40 percent of the U.S. population, traveled through Grand Central Terminal. That same year, the Ice Cream Merchandising Institute promoted a sundae served at one of the terminal's dining facilities.

**2 scoops** vanilla ice cream
**3 ounces** hot fudge
**3 ounces** marshmallow syrup
salted peanuts, whole

Place two scoops of vanilla ice cream side by side on an oval dish. Cover one scoop with hot fudge, the other with marshmallow. Layer salted peanuts overall.

From *Let's Eat Ice Cream* (1947): "If you're making a nut sundae, cover the entire surface with dry nuts, sprinkled with a spoon.

During the golden age of train travel in the 1930s and 1940s, Grand Central's Biltmore Room was known as the "Kissing Room." When the 20th Century Limited arrived from the West Coast, passengers would get off the train and greet their loved ones here with kisses and hugs.

# halloween

Candy corn was created in the 1880s by George Renninger of the Wunderlee Candy Company, the three colors meant to mimic corn. Each piece is approximately the size of a whole kernel of corn, as if it fell off a ripe or dried ear of corn. The traditional Halloween candy is usually tri-colored with a yellow base, orange center, and white tip, although the color combinations may vary.

**2 scoops** vanilla ice cream
**4 ounces** chocolate syrup
whipped cream
candy corn kernels
maraschino cherry

Into a tulip sundae glass put 1 ounce of chocolate syrup. Add 2 scoops of vanilla ice cream. Cover with remaining chocolate syrup. Top with whipped cream, layer with candy corn, and garnish with cherry.

{ Into a tulip sundae glass put 1 ounce of chocolate syrup. Add 2 scoops of vanilla ice cream. Cover with remaining chocolate syrup. Top with whipped cream, layer with candy corn, and garnish with cherry. }

From The Bulletin of Pharmacy (1919): "The sundae cup should be selected carefully. They are to be had in great variety in glass, silver and china. Some are clumsy, some are dainty, while others are of a very serviceable type. Silver cups do not break and so long as they shine they are all right, but when a dispenser tries to use a bent, twisted, dented and plate, he injures his business."

# happy thought sundae

Housed in an 1856 building listed on the National Register of Historic Places, the Wilton Candy Kitchen (Wilton, Iowa) dates back to 1910 when a young Greek immigrant named Gus Napoulos arrived in town to make chocolates and sell ice cream sodas and sundaes. The Napolous family still serves the vintage recipe, double-icecream, double-fruit, whipped-cream and cherry-on-top sundae, decorated with miniature American and Greek flags to honor their national and ethnic heritage.

**2 scoops** vanilla ice cream
**1/2** banana, peeled, sliced into wheels
**4 ounces** crushed strawberries
whipped cream
maraschino cherry

Dip 2 scoops of vanilla ice cream onto an oval dish. In the center between the two, add the crushed strawberries. Place banana wheels around the ice creams. Top with whipped cream and garnish with maraschino cherry.

{ From *The Bulletin of Pharmacy* (1917): "Do not stick the spoon into the glass or ice cream. Hand a clean spoon to your customer, holding it in the center, handle foremost." }

From The Pacific Drug Review (1920): *"When experimenting with new dishes, always take notes and make diagrams. Many a great combination has been lost because this simple rule was not obeyed."*

# harry truman sundae

The year was 1898. Harry Truman was 14 and a high school student when he went to work for at J. H. Clinton's drugstore on the town square in Independence, Missouri. Young Harry had to turn the ice cream freezer for each day's output, dispense ice cream behind the soda fountain, carry out the trash, and sweep up. The local soda jerk who grew up to become the thirty-third President of the United States had a personal favorite, still served at Clinton's: chocolate ice cream with butterscotch sauce (no nuts, no whipped cream).

**2 scoops** chocolate ice cream
**4 ounces** hot butterscotch

Into a tulip sundae glass put 1 ounce of the butterscotch. Add the chocolate ice cream. Cover with remaining butterscotch.

{ In 1938, the soda fountain staff at the University of Michigan rejected the term "soda jerks," instead calling themselves "fountaineers." }

*An American folk hero, the craftsman behind the fountain was called soda clerk, dispenser, "the professor," or soda jerk (after the jerking action the server would use on the soda fountain handle when drawing soda water).*

# hay stack sundae

A visionary named Gail Borden established the nation's first milk condensery in Burrville, Connecticut, in 1857. By 1928, the company had expanded to all regions of the country selling the Borden brand of milk products, including ice cream. In the 1940s, when Elsie the Cow became the company symbol, a study showed that more people recognized Elsie than President Harry Truman. An early manual for soda fountain operators produced by the company featured the Hay Stack as a "Special Sundae Formula."

**2 scoops** vanilla ice cream
**3 tablespoons** crushed strawberries
shredded coconut, toasted
maraschino cherry

Into a tulip sundae glass put 1 tablespoon crushed strawberries. Add 2 scoops vanilla ice cream. Cover with remaining strawberries. Top with coconut and garnish with cherry.

{ **From** *The Pacific Drug Review* (1920): "The foundation of perfect mixing lies in an accurate knowledge of each ingredient used and the amount required to make each drink or sundae." }

*In certain sections of New England, the sundae was called a "throw-over," a portion of ice cream with some dressing "thrown over" it, with the result anything but pleasant to the eye.*

# high school special

Pop Tate's Chocklit Shoppe is a fictional soda shop created by Bob Montana as a setting for the characters in his *Archie* comic strip. Tate's soda fountain was based on real-life locations frequented by teenagers in Haverhill, Massachusetts, during the 1930s. The character of Pop Tate was inspired by the Greek immigrant owner of these Haverhill soda shops. In the years 1936 to 1939, when Montana went to high school in Haverhill, he would join his friends at the counter and make sketches on napkins.

**2 scoops** vanilla ice cream
**2 tablespoons** chopped cherries in syrup
**3 ounces** marshmallow syrup
whipped cream
Spanish peanuts

Dip scoops of vanilla ice cream side by side in an oval dish. Cover one scoop with the chopped cherries, and cover the other with marshmallow. Top with whipped cream and layer with peanuts.

From *The Retail Druggist* (1920): "When you advertise a special, let it be one of such quality that you can safely guarantee it to give satisfaction."

From The Pacific Drug Review (1918): "Choose some drink or sundae that you want to make a run on; let two or three of the most popular high school girls and boys who come into your store try it; ask their opinions, and If they like it you can be pretty nearly certain they're going to tell the rest of the crowd about it, and before you know it, you will have calls for it regularly."

# hoboken sundae

The locals call it "Schnak's." A Hoboken, New Jersey institution, Schnackenberg's Luncheonette opened in 1931, its owner one of the German immigrants who populated this city on the west bank of the Hudson River (across from Manhattan). The soda fountain offers a snapshot into an earlier era, which is probably why a scene from Leonardo DiCaprio's film, *The Basketball Diaries*, was shot here. You can still squeeze into one of the narrow two-person booths, sized for the hips and thighs of an earlier generation, for a sundae connected to the city.

**2 scoops** chocolate ice cream
**4 ounces** crushed pineapple
whipped cream
maraschino cherry

Dip scoops of chocolate ice cream onto an oval dish. In the center between the two, add the crushed pineapple. Top with whipped cream and garnish with cherry.

{ The foundation of perfect mixing lies in an accurate knowledge of each ingredient used and the amount required to make each drink or sundae. }

From The Pacific Drug Review (1920): *"Serve fruit salad sundaes, fruited lemonade, made from fresh lemons. Feature fresh fruit salad, topped with sweet whipped cream, and served with a sweet biscuit on the side. There are innumerable ways to serve this healthful dessert."*

# home style sundae

*The Soda Fountain Handbook* had some sound advice for World War II era fountain managers on the homefront: "If you have an inherent talent for improvisation, your greatest outlet is in the field dealing with sundaes. With just a few simple syrups and the variety of toppings you have on your soda fountain, you can turn out an exhaustive array of possible combinations." And, one good rule to remember: PUT IN PLENTY OF ICE CREAM.

**2 scoops** vanilla ice cream
**1 ring** sliced pineapple
**4 ounces** hot butterscotch
Brazil nuts

On a china saucer place the pineapple ring. Dip 2 scoops of vanilla ice cream onto the pineapple. Cover with butterscotch. Sprinkle Brazil nuts over the top.

According to *White's Vest Pocket Sundae Formulary*, **a similar fountain formula was called the Sunshine Sundae.**

*From* The Pacific Drug Review *(1920): "The plain sundae consists of the portion of ice cream with a proper amount of dressing carefully poured over it. Most dispensers use too much, with the result that the average sundae is nauseatingly sweet."*

# hot butterscotch sundae

Bailey's was a lovely old Boston ice cream shop, opened in 1873 by candymakers John B. Bailey and D.H. Page, originally selling candy bears, chocolates, and other confections. Bailey's of Boston became an ice cream parlor, eventually with as many as a dozen locations in and around the city. It was the home of legendary butterscotch sundaes, served in silver-plated pedestal dishes set on small round silver plates to catch the rich sauce which always dripped down from the dish. The secret was a base of coffee ice cream, cutting the sweetness of the sauce, and a final crowning of whipped cream and walnuts.

**2 scoops** coffee ice cream
**4 ounces** hot butterscotch
whipped cream
walnuts, chopped

Into a tulip sundae glass put 1 ounce of butterscotch. Add 2 scoops of coffee ice cream. Cover with remaining butterscotch. Top with whipped cream sprinkle with the walnuts.

{ Pop artist Andy Warhol on the Beverly Hills shopping district: "Rodeo Drive is a giant Butterscotch Sundae." }

*The venerable Bailey's of Boston was once an important stop on any shopping trip to Jordan Marsh, Gilchrist's, R.H. Stearns or other long-forgotten downtown department stores.*

# hot fudge sundae

The world's first hot fudge sundaes were served at Clarence Clifton Brown's Hollywood, California, ice cream parlor in 1906. Your server scooped vanilla ice cream into a silver goblet, then added a dollop of whipped cream and a sprinkling of chopped roasted almonds. Small brown ceramic pitchers filled with hot fudge were kept in a hot water bath until an order was placed, then served on the side. You could pour it over the top of the ice cream in one fell swoop, or parcel it out over the course of eating your sundae.

**2 scoops** vanilla ice cream
**6 ounces** hot fudge sauce
whipped cream
salted almonds, chopped

Into a tulip sundae glass put 1 ounce of hot fudge. Add 2 scoops of vanilla ice cream. Top with whipped cream and sprinkle with the almonds. Fill a small pitcher with remaining hot fudge and serve on the side.

Situated half a block from Mann's Chinese Theater, C.C. Brown's became a popular hangout for celebrities like Mary Pickford, Joan Crawford and Bob Hope as well as regular folks looking for a treat after a night out at the movies.

From St. Louis-based Meyer Brothers Druggist (1918): "The boy of today knows that the girl of today wants the dishes of today (ice cream) whether the weather is hot or cold, says the Soda Dispenser. In the winter she likes it best with a nice warm dressing. Install a fudge set if you have not already done so."

# hot penuche sundae

Steve Herrell was the first person to grind up Heath Bars, Reese's Peanut Butter Cups, Oreos, and other name-brand confections and mix them into ice cream. He introduced "smoosh-ins" or "mixins" to ice cream culture when he opened Steve's Ice Cream in Somerville, Massachusetts, in 1973. Contrary to F. Scott Fitzgerald's famous maxim that "there are no second acts in American life," in 1980 Steve launched Herrell's Ice Cream, expanding upon his formulas, including the favorite New England confection, penuche, as a sundae topping.

**2 scoops** vanilla ice cream
**4 ounces** hot penuche
whipped cream
maraschino cherry

Into a tulip sundae glass put 1 ounce hot penuche. Add 2 scoops of vanilla ice cream. Cover with remaining hot penuche. Top with whipped cream and garnish with cherry.

{ Penuche is best-known as a fudge-like candy made from brown sugar, butter, and milk, using no flavorings except for vanilla. Its flavor is said to be reminiscent of caramel. }

*Years ago, when Steve Herrell was asked what his favorite flavor was, he replied, "Vanilla." When asked why, he said that vanilla was the base for all of his other flavors, and if a company couldn't make a good vanilla they probably couldn't make a good anything else.*

# i.c.u. sundae

In 1914, *The Spatula Soda Water Guide* attempted to define a sundae for the drug store trade: "A sundae is a dish of ice cream over which is poured a given syrup or crushed fruit, with or without nuts or whipped cream. The sundae is so elaborated that it becomes almost anything with ice cream in it as long as it is not a drink." In fountains of the era, the name I.C.U. (short for "I see you") lent a special aura of quality to a fancified Strawberry Sundae.

**2 scoops** vanilla ice cream
**3 tablespoons** crushed strawberries
salted almonds, chopped
whipped cream
cinnamon powder

Into a tulip sundae glass put 1 tablespoon crushed strawberries. Add 2 scoops of vanilla ice cream. Cover with remaining strawberries. Sprinkle almonds on top and add whipped cream. Dust with cinnamon.

{ While the term "sundae" is universally known to the profession, the sundae possesses many local names applied in other sections to entirely different fountain preparations. In some parts of the South it was called a "lollypop." }

*While it is customary to decorate each sundae and dish of ice cream with a cherry, a strawberry may be used instead, selecting sound, fully ripe, dark red berries of medium size. The service is dainty and sundaes thus decorated look attractive and the public likes the change.*

# jack and jill sundae

A "freezing and dispensing machine," invented by Harry Oltz of Hammond, Indiana, designed to freeze ice milk mix and hold it until drawn out through a specially designed faucet, created soft-serve ice cream – hallmark of the Dairy Queen franchise. Obtaining exclusive rights to the machine, John McCullough and Herb Noble opened the first Dairy Queen in Joliet, Illinois, with the new product and new freezer. That spark of imagination has grown into an international company with more than 5,200 stores worldwide. An early offering was the Dairy Queen version of a Black and White Sundae.

**1 scoop** vanilla ice cream
**2 ounces** chocolate syrup
**2 ounces** marshmallow syrup
whipped cream
maraschino cherry

Into a tulip sundae glass add 1 scoop vanilla ice cream. Cover one side with the chocolate syrup, the other side with the marshmallow. Top with whipped cream and garnish with cherry.

During the 1950s and 1960s, Dairy Queens in the small towns of the Midwestern and Southern United States were a center of social life.

*Take the sundae cup in the left hand and the disher in the right. Fill the disher just full enough to round its base slightly. Learn to force the ice cream in the cup so that the portion sits evenly in the dish, and to do it without getting the ice cream on the outside of the dish.*

# joe sent me

There are few things in this world that go together as well as chocolate and strawberries, as confirmed by the Joe Sent Me sundae at the Sweet Dreams Café in Stroudsburg, Pennsylvania, an historic town in the Pocono foothills. The Sweet Dreams fountain inherited the formula (and the name) from legendary Jahn's, the defunct chain of New York City ice cream parlors that coined sundae names like Boilermaker, Awful Awful, Suicide Frappe, and Screwball's Delight.

**2 scoops** vanilla ice cream
**3 ounces** hot fudge
**2 tablespoons** crushed strawberries
whipped cream
maraschino cherry

Into a tulip sundae glass put 1 ounce hot fudge. Add 2 scoops of vanilla ice cream. Cover with remaining hot fudge, then crushed strawberries. Top with whipped cream and garnish with cherry.

The chief requisites necessary to the serving of a good sundae are pure, high-grade syrups and crushed fruits and a good grade of ice cream.

*Instead of using strawberry syrup from a pump, obtain a strawberry pulp syrup, permitting the crushed or ground pulp of the fruit to remain in the syrup, and serve it from pitchers.*

# june bride sundae

Historically, June is the most popular month for weddings. The reason has less to do with weather and more to with Juno, the ancient Roman goddess of marriage. Romans chose to honor her by tying the knot in June, and like a lot of traditions, this one stuck. There was a practical side to June weddings as well, and practicality also shows up quite a bit in rituals and traditions. A marriage in June could result in a conception early enough so that a wife wouldn't be too full with child to not be able to help out during the harvest.

**2 scoops** chocolate ice cream
**3 tablespoons** crushed strawberries
whipped cream
walnuts, chopped
whole fresh strawberry

Into a tulip sundae glass put 1 tablespoon crushed strawberries. Add 2 scoops of chocolate ice cream. Cover with remaining crushed strawberries. Top with whipped cream and garnish with whole strawberry.

In most regions of North America, the best of locally and naturally grown strawberries are in season beginning in mid-June.

*The best way to store strawberries is to refrigerate them unwashed with the green hulls (tops) intact. Place in a shallow pan lined with paper towel, top with additional paper towel and cover with plastic wrap. When ready to use, wash just before serving with a light spray of water, gently pat dry and remove hulls.*

# knickbocker glory

The term "knickerbocker" comes from the surname of Diedrich Knickerbocker, the fictional narrator of *A History of New York* by Washington Irving. In the early 19th century it became a nickname for Manhattan residents. By the early 20th century the name was attached to a confection of ice cream, jelly, and fruit alternated in a tall glass and topped with kinds of syrup, nuts and whipped cream. Originally served in New York, the dish was adopted by the British. This exhibition of sundae-maker art is adapted from *The Dispenser's Formulary* (1915).

**3 scoops** vanilla ice cream
**2 ounces** chocolate syrup
**1 tablespoon** crushed raspberries
**1 tablespoon** crushed cherries
whipped cream
walnuts, chopped
maraschino cherry

Into a parfait glass put 1 ounce chocolate syrup. Add 1 scoop of vanilla ice cream and cover with 1 tablespoon of the crushed raspberries. Add 1 scoop of vanilla ice cream and cover with remaining chocolate syrup. Add 1 scoop of vanilla ice cream and cover with 1 tablespoon of the crushed cherries. Top with the whipped cream, sprinkle with dry walnuts, and garnish with the whole cherry.

*The Brits claim that the name Knickerbocker Glory is drawn from "knickerbockers,"*
*a type of long trouser traditionally worn by young children (but particularly young boys).*
*"Glory" reflects the typical reaction of a child presented with such a dessert.*

# la royale sundae

Menu cards referred to sundaes as "Parfaits Américaines" at the Pharmacie Britannique on the rue Royale in Paris. According to popular notion, this soda fountain was the French connection responsible for the term "royale" at soda fountains everywhere. The "royale" was a special, and advice to the trade in American Druggist magazine warned: "Be sure that your special is a good one; make it one that is likely to please the greater number of your customers. Possibly it would be better to have two specials. Tastes and desires differ, you know."

**1 scoop** vanilla ice cream
**1 scoop** chocolate ice cream
**1 slice** sponge cake
**2 tablespoons** crushed pineapple
**2 tablespoons** crushed strawberries
whipped cream
maraschino cherry

Place sponge cake on a flat dish. Add 1 scoop of vanilla and 1 scoop of chocolate ice creams. Cover vanilla ice cream with the crushed pineapple, chocolate ice cream with the crushed strawberries. Top with whipped cream and garnish with cherry.

According to *White's Vest Pocket Sundae Formulary*, **a similar fountain formula was called the Dutchess Sundae..**

From The New York Times (2004): "The French may have given refinement to ice cream with their coupes and parfaits, but it took American excess and ingenuity to create the sundae — as messy and irresistible as democracy itself."

# lola sundae

A 1914 issue of *The Bulletin of Pharmacy* offers instructions for strawberry topping: "Prepare the fresh berries as in making crushed fruit, mashing the pulp as fine as possible, add as much sugar as will dissolve in the fruit in the cold, then strain through muslin or very fine gauze. This makes a delicious syrup and has a distinctive taste, differing from that of the syrup made by the hot process. Only the richest flavored berries should be used."

**1 scoop** strawberry ice cream
**1 scoop** vanilla ice cream
**4 tablespoons** crushed strawberries
whipped cream
whole fresh strawberry

Into a tulip sundae glass put 1 tablespoon of the crushed strawberries. Add 1 scoop of strawberry ice cream and cover with 1 tablespoon of the crushed strawberries. Add 1 scoop of vanilla ice cream and cover with remaining crushed strawberries. Top with whipped cream and garnish with the whole strawberry.

Even if you have to give a fancy price for the fruit it will pay to feature fresh strawberry combinations during strawberry season.

*While it is customary to decorate each sundae and dish of ice cream with a cherry, use a strawberry instead, selecting sound, fully ripe, dark red berries of medium size. The service is dainty and sundaes thus decorated look attractive and the public likes the change. Vary the monotony in every way you can.*

# maple walnut sundae

In April of 1947, Carl Sponseller opened a frozen custard store in a former gas station on Route 1 in Fredericksburg, Virginia, the busiest north-south travel route in the eastern United States at the time. Although the country's Interstate system has bypassed Carl's, people still wait in long lines for ice cream churned out by vintage Electo-Freeze machines. Ordering is reminiscent of the *Seinfeld* "Soup Nazi" episode. Customer-enforced protocol calls for one to approach the counter with money in hand, order decisively and step aside quickly. Carl's Maple Walnut Sundae is a local favorite.

**2 scoops** vanilla ice cream
**3 tablespoons** wet walnuts
whipped cream
**1** walnut half

Into a tulip sundae glass put 1 tablespoon wet walnuts. Add 2 scoops of vanilla ice cream. Cover with remaining wet walnuts. Top with whipped cream and garnish with walnut half.

> From The Retail Druggist (1920): "A small dish heaping full may look as though you gave more for the money than the same amount would in a larger dish."

*Getting Away from the Ten-cent Sundae: Offering "something special" at many fountains takes the form of dressings containing nut meats in some form or other, and the Maple Walnut Sundae is suggested for menus where the owners believe a price of fifteen cents a portion is justified:*

64

# merry widow sundae

In 1919, W. O. Rigby produced *The Reliable Candy Teacher*, including a guide to "Sundaes and Fancy Ice Cream Dishes." For serving a fountain sundae, he suggests: "A china or silver cup should be used, serving on trays to match. Or glass serving dishes can be used. A small glass of ice water should always be served with each order." Included among Rigby's formulas was a sundae named for an operetta that filled concert halls in the early 20th century.

1 **scoop** vanilla ice cream
1 **tablespoon** crushed cherries
1 **tablespoon** crushed pineapple
whipped cream
maraschino cherry

Into a tulip sundae glass add 1 scoop of vanilla ice cream. Cover with crushed cherries and crushed pineapple. Top with whipped cream and garnish with the whole cherry.

From *Let's Sell Ice Cream* (1947): "Ice cream is a nutritious food – be proud to serve it."

From The Pacific Drug Review (1922): "Make sure that nothing is served at your fountain that you would not order yourself. This does not mean that you must like everything you serve, but rather that its quality is such that you would not hesitate to order. Back "good sundae" with "acceptable service" and it will make the other fellow's coin jump your way."

# merry-go-round sundae

In 1919, Hans Petersen founded an ice cream institution in Oak Park, the Chicago suburb with the highest concentration of houses or buildings anywhere designed and built by Frank Lloyd Wright, the dean of American architecture. Petersen's still retains a vintage character, serving a playful sundae inspired by the amusement park rides in old Chicago.

**1 large scoop** vanilla ice cream
**4 ounces** chocolate syrup
animal crackers
small paper parasol

On a round, flat dish, dip the scoop of vanilla ice cream onto the center. Cover with the chocolate syrup. Arrange animal crackers around the ice cream. Place the paper parasol at the top.

{ From a 1917 issue of *The Bulletin of Pharmacy*: "Some soda jerkers are born to be artistic, others have to learn to be. There is a knack, natural or acquired, in decorating those things that require decoration so that they look tempting." }

*At Petersen's, waiters jot down jot down "chocolate O" on their order pads for a chocolate soda, and "chocolate U" for a sundae (Can you crack the code?).*

# missouri sundae

In 1942, leaders in the soda fountain industry brought together their combined thinking and knowledge in management course called *The Soda Fountain Handbook*. Offered from a list of formulas "to indicate the possibilities confronting the manager who has the initiative and the intelligence to make his fountain noted for sundaes," was the marriage of chocolate and strawberry in a dish named for the "Show Me" state.

**2 scoops** chocolate ice cream
**3 tablespoons** crushed strawberries
whipped cream
whole fresh strawberry

Into a tulip sundae glass put 1 tablespoon crushed strawberries. Add 2 scoops of chocolate ice cream. Cover with remaining crushed strawberries. Top with whipped cream and garnish with whole strawberry.

The reverse of this formula, strawberry ice cream with chocolate syrup is called the Buddie Sundae.

*From* The Retail Druggist *(1920): "A whole strawberry placed on the apex of the ice cream adds little to the cost but a great deal to the artistic appearance of the confection. And it makes it a whole lot easier for the druggist to ask for and get the better price."*

# monte cristo sundae

By the mid-1930s, Hollywood had already produced five motion pictures based on the exploits of the Count of Monte Cristo, the swashbuckling character created in literature by Alexandre Dumas. The Count became inspiration for both a sandwich and a sundae at luncheonettes. Menus offered a combo of ham and turkey (or chicken), dipped in egg and fried like French toast, then for dessert a caramel sundae, topped with cashews and a chocolate shot – both named for the French hero.

**2 scoops** vanilla ice cream
**4 ounces** caramel sauce
whipped cream
salted cashews, whole
**1 ounce** chocolate syrup

Into a tulip sundae glass put 1 ounce of caramel sauce. Add 2 scoops of vanilla ice cream. Cover with remaining caramel. Top with whipped cream and layer with cashews. Finish with chocolate shot.

{ Few famous novels have been filmed as often as *The Count of Monte Cristo*, and few versions are as enjoyable as the 1934 adaptation starring British actor Robert Donat in his only U.S. picture. }

*Cashews are found growing on trees or "bushes" near the equator. The Spanish word for cashew, maranon, originated from Maranho, Brazil, one of the first regions where the Spanish observed cashews growing in the wild. The native Brazilian cashew is the largest, sweetest and whitest cashew.*

# mud pie

Remember the coffee shop in *Pulp Fiction*? Scenes that opened and closed the film were shot on location at Pann's, the futuristic "googie-style" architectural wonder on LaTijera Boulevard in Los Angeles. Since 1958, the Panagopoulos family has served breakfast, lunch, and dinner with desserts that include a West Coast version of the Mississippi Mud Pie, a sundae resting on a slice of chocolate cake. The dessert was created in the 1950s with a dense cake said to resemble the banks of the Mississippi River.

**1 slice** chocolate cake
**1 scoop** vanilla ice cream
**4 ounces** ho t fudge
whipped cream
maraschino cherry

Place slice of cake on a flat dish. Add one scoop of vanilla ice cream. Cover with hot fudge. Top with whipped cream and garnish with cherry.

{ Chocolate cake crumbs become "blacktop" in the Pot Hole
Sundae, a creation of Gifford's in Skohegan, Maine. }

Howard Johnson's Fountain Service Manual *offers directions on scooping ice cream:* "Hold the scoop firmly, with your thumb under the release. The closer your hand is to the head of the scoop, the better leverage you have."

# muddle sundae

James Papageorge arrived in the United States as a nine-year-old stowaway from Tripoli, Greece, in 1904. He landed in Chicago where, with hard work and determination, he earned a living by scooping ice cream at a soda fountain and selling fruit at a fruit stand. By 1920, he had saved enough money to buy Gayety's, an ice cream parlor and candy store nestled next to the Gayety Theater on Chicago's South Side. The vaudeville and feature picture showplace is long gone, but the Papageorge family continues Gayety's tradition in suburban Lansing, notable for serving the Muddle Sundae.

**2 scoops** vanilla ice cream
**3 ounces** caramel sauce
**4 ounces** hot fudge
whipped cream
salted pecans, chopped
maraschino cherry

Into a tulip sundae glass put 1 ounce hot fudge. Add 2 scoops of vanilla ice cream. Cover with 3 ounces caramel. Top with whipped cream. Sprinkle with pecans and garnish with cherry. Fill a small pitcher with remaining hot fudge and serve on the side.

Hot fudge should be kept at a temperature high enough to insure its being in an easy-to- pour state, yet not hot enough to cause it to "sugar" after standing a few hours.

*Ingrid Bergman, already an established movie star in Europe, came to New York in 1939 when she was twenty-four. She loved hot fudge sundaes so much that she alarmed her American hosts.*

# mutt and jeff

The very first newspaper comic strip, created by Bud Fisher in 1907, "Mutt and Jeff" remained in syndication until 1982, over time drawn by several cartoonists, chiefly Al Smith who produced the strip for nearly 50 years. The strip's waning circulation got a shot in the arm during the 1930s when it inspired an ice cream sundae, then again in the 1950s when President Eisenhower sang its praises. Themes often revolved around the get-rich-quick schemes of tall, dimwitted Mutt, with half-pint Jeff as a sometimes unwilling partner.

**2 scoops** vanilla ice cream
**4 ounces** chocolate syrup
**2 malted** milk balls
shredded coconut, toasted

Dip one large scoop and one small scoop of vanilla ice cream side by side on an oval dish. Top each scoop with a malted milk ball. Ladle the chocolate syrup over the ice cream, then sprinkle with toasted coconut.

{ Over the years, a similar fountain formula has been called the Laurel and Hardy or the Abbott and Costello. }

*The Overland Candy Company introduced a malted milk candy product called Giants in 1939. In 1947, Overland merged with Leaf Brands and reintroduced malted milk balls in 1949 under the name of "Whoppers."*

# new york sundae

The Waldorf-Astoria became part of the New York culture in the early 20th century with a popular expression, "Meet Me at the Hyphen." In the Waldorf kitchen, famed head chef Louis De Gouy invented a slightly more luxurious version of the Strawberry Sundae and christened it after his city. With the addition of chopped pistachios, the dish became a Four-Hundred Sundae, named for the city's wealthiest, most powerful social group, leading to the generation of such lists as the Forbes 400.

**1 scoop** vanilla ice cream
**1 ounce** claret syrup
**2 tablespoons** crushed strawberries
whipped cream
1 large fresh strawberry, in season

Dip vanilla ice cream into a champagne coupe. Over the ice cream pour claret syrup, then cover with crushed strawberries. Top with whipped cream and garnish with strawberry.

{ From *The Pacific Drug Review* (1920): "The chief requisites necessary to the serving of a good sundae are pure, high-grade syrups and crushed fruits and a good grade of ice cream." }

From The Pacific Drug Review (1920): "The chief requisites necessary to the serving of a good sundae are pure, high-grade syrups and crushed fruits and a good grade of ice cream."

# oriental parfait

From *Let's Sell Ice Cream* (1947): "The parfait is one of the most glamorous dishes made at the soda fountain or ice cream department. The imagination and skill of the dispenser combine to create a colorful effect of ice cream and toppings, like an ice cream rainbow. Common practice is to 'layer' firm ice cream and toppings to produce a pleasing combination of flavors."

**1 scoop vanilla ice cream**
**1 scoop** chocolate ice cream
**1 scoop** strawberry ice cream
**1 tablespoon** crushed pineapple
**2 tablespoons** chopped cherries
**1 tablespoon** wet walnuts
whipped cream
dry walnuts, chopped
maraschino cherry

Into a parfait glass put the crushed pineapple. Add the vanilla ice cream and cover with 1 tablespoon of the chopped cherries. Add the chocolate ice cream and cover with the wet walnuts. Add the strawberry ice cream and cover with 1 tablespoon of the chopped cherries. Top with the whipped cream, sprinkle with dry walnuts, and garnish with the whole cherry.

From The Bulletin of Pharmacy (1916): "The layer parfait is sometimes dispensed in four, five, or even six layers, but the more layers the more work, and the more time consumed in dispensing. Three layers work very well; a layer of ice cream at the bottom of the glass, then a layer of the added ingredient, with a layer of ice cream to top off."

# peach melba sundae

From *The Bulletin of Pharmacy* (1919): "To introduce a new sundae, a Florida soda fountain operator had circulars distributed around town offering the sundae free to every child under seven years of age who would come in and ask for it, using this sentence correctly : 'I want to try Mr. Lester's new Peach Melba.' If the sentence was repeated correctly, the child was given the sundae free. Of course, children of this age would have to be coached by their elders and thus the advertising value was realized as the older folks become familiar with the name and the new sundae. In practically all cases, the youngsters were accompanied by their parents, or some older member of the family, and this was also a drawing card for the store."

**1 scoop** vanilla ice cream
**1/2** peach, pitted and poached
**3 ounces** melba syrup
whipped cream
sweet cracker

Into a wide sundae goblet put the peach half. Add 1 scoop of vanilla ice cream. Cover with the melba syrup. Top with whipped cream and serve with the sweet cracker.

Salty crackers could accompany chocolate, coffee and malt flavors, but only a sweet cracker is properly served with a fruit sundae.

*The original Peach Melba was legendary French chef Escoffier's most famous dessert recipe created for Australian opera star Nellie Melba when she was staying at London's Savoy Hotel in 1893.*

# philadelphia coffee sundae

In 1861, a Quaker schoolteacher named Louis Dubois Bassett set out to make high-quality ice creams on his rural New Jersey farm. In 1893, Bassett's Ice Cream opened up shop in Philadelphia's Reading Terminal Market where they have remained ever since. In 1866, William Breyer started hand-cranking ice cream in his Kensington kitchen and selling it to neighbors. Within months, he was delivering his ice cream to a growing number of customers in a horsedrawn wagon. The accessibility of fresh milk and cream from farms in and around Philadelphia led to a proliferation of nearly fifty ice cream manufacturers in the city at one time. Bassett's, Breyer's and other Philadelphia ice cream makers refrained from using egg yolks to stabilize their product, using only cream, sugar and sometimes milk. Philadelphia-style ice cream, made without eggs, became a national phenomenon.

**1 scoop** coffee ice cream
**4 ounces** marshmallow syrup

Dip 1 scoop of coffee ice cream into a small sundae glass. Cover with marshmallow.

Sundae ingredients took a while to become standardized; as late as 1910 one magazine defined the sundae as "a mixture of ice cream, soda-water, and raspberry juice.

From The Confectioners Journal (1907): "Every customer after a sundae wants a glass of water, although most dispensers don't seem to think so or else try to forget it. One Philadelphia drug store had a water cooler placed near the fountain, as customers find it easier to serve themselves than to ask for ice water."

# pike's peak sundae

Lt. Zebulon Montgomery Pike discovered the mountain in 1806 on an excursion to explore the western Great Plains and the Rocky Mountains in Colorado. Pike originally named the mountain "Grand Peak," but cartographers labeled it "Pikes Peak" on their maps. Pike's only attempt to climb the mountain was unsuccessful due to a cold November storm, and Pike later predicted that "no one would ever reach the summit. Pike's Peak became the most visited mountain in North America and the second most visited mountain in the world behind Japan's Mount Fuji.

**2 scoops** chocolate ice cream
**4 ounces** chocolate syrup
shredded coconut
maraschino cherry

Into a tulip sundae glass put 1 ounce of chocolate syrup. Add 2 scoops of chocolate ice cream. Cover with remaining chocolate syrup. Top with shredded coconut and garnish with cherry.

The Pike's Peak trail climbs 7500 vertical feel in just under 13 miles to the top. The forest service estimates that a round trip hiking will take approximately 16 hours.

From Rigby's Reliable Candy Teacher (1921): "A twelve-to-the-quart scoop is used for plain ice cream, sundaes and college ices, and a sixteen-to-thequart scoop for ice cream sodas and banana royals. Sometimes a twenty-to-thequart scoop is used for banana splits and other fancy fruit specialties."

# pink lady sundae

Marshmallow came into its own during the heyday of drugstore soda fountains and confectionery stores. Back then, plain marshmallow sundaes were big sellers, and chocolate-marshmallow sundaes were standard on most menus. Originated during the 1950s by Clinton Roe, Jr. at Clint's Ice Cream in Los Altos, California, the Pink Lady Sundae featured marshmallow colored pink and flavored with a small amount of peppermint extract.

**2 scoops** vanilla ice cream
**4 ounces** marshmallow, colored with strawberry juice, flavored with peppermint extract
whipped cream
dry walnuts, chopped

Into a tulip sundae glass put 1 ounce of marshmallow. Add 2 scoops of chocolate ice cream. Cover with remaining marshmallow. Top with whipped cream, sprinkle with walnuts, and garnish with cherry.

DISPENSING TIP: Thick marshmallow is not the easiest topping to pour from a ladle. So, simply let it dribble off the bottom of the ladle.

According to Bryce Thomson, editor of The Sundae School Newsletter: "Marshmallow is the most versatile of all because it combines so well with other toppings, syrups, and nuts. Old-time professional soda jerks used it as a second or third topping to transform a 'regular' sundae into a 'special' sundae, commanding a higher price."

# polka-dot sundae

The 1943 film, *The Gang's All Here*, directed and choreographed by Busby Berkeley, features Alice Faye singing "The Polka Dot Polka," once and for always linking the lively folk dance to the whimsical clothing design. When Polish immigrants arrived in America with their accordion music, the population was inspired to dance. Dots and the dance became all the rage as the playful, bouncing pattern imitated the polka's upbeat tempo. Soda fountain operators connected the dots and came up with a Polka-Dot Sundae.

**2 scoops** peppermint ice cream
**4 ounces** chocolate syrup
whipped cream
maraschino cherry

Into a tulip sundae glass put 1 ounce chocolate syrup. Add 2 scoops of peppermint ice cream. Cover with remaining chocolate syrup. Top with whipped cream and decorate with a chocolate shot.

{ From the J. Hungerford Smith *Fountain Formula Book*: "Imagination and skill properly applied to sundaes will not only lend glamour to your fountain but dollars to your pocket." }

*In 1941, Drug Store Management, a magazine for the trade, scolded fountain operators for permitting the use of slang in their establishments, pointing out that "it tends to reduce the formality of the occasion and may perhaps suggest a lack of respect for the customer's order."*

# popcorn sundae

A 1916 issue of *The Bulletin of Pharmacy* offered a "palate tickler" called the Chocolate Popcorn Sundae, using "well-popped corn from which all the hard unpopped kernels have been removed." The magazine assured soda fountain operators that "You will find few sundaes that will look, taste or sell better than this one.

**2 scoops** chocolate ice cream
**6 ounces** hot fudge
pop corn
whipped cream
maraschino cherry

Dip 2 scoops of chocolate ice cream onto an oval dish. Cover with 3 ounces of hot fudge. Sprinkle pop corn very liberally and cover with remaining hot fudge. Top with whipped cream and garnish with cherry.

During the Depression, popcorn, at 10 cents a bag, was one of the few luxuries poorer families could afford; so while other businesses failed, the popcorn business thrived.

*"The use of ice cream at the soda fountain in various sections of the country has increased enormously," according to* Confectioners Journal *(1916). "It has become so that it is no unusual thing in certain localities for a confectioner or even a druggist to run regularly six or eight kinds of ice cream."*

# prom parfait

Proms first began in the elite colleges of the Northeast, taking their cue from the debutante balls of the rich and well-bred. Middle class parents admired the poise and composure of debutantes and their escorts and began to institute formal dances as a means of instilling social skills and etiquette in their children. The dances were strictly chaperoned and were often restricted to only the senior class. Soda fountain operators appropriated the name for a well-bred parfait.

**1 scoop** strawberry ice cream
**1 scoop** vanilla ice cream
**2 tablespoons crushed strawberries**
**1 tablespoon** crushed pineapple
whipped cream
maraschino cherry

Into a parfait glass put 1 tablespoon crushed strawberries. Add the strawberry ice cream and cover with the remaining crushed strawberries. Add the vanilla ice cream and cover with the crushed pineapple. Top with whipped cream and garnish with cherry.

{ From the J. Hungerford Smith *Fountain Formula Book*: "A parfait
is distinctly a "fancy" dish, therefore, not a low price service." }

From The Druggists Circular (*1933*): *"The strawberry, shaped by nature in conical
form, is admirably adapted to topping a sundae. It looks well and gives the
customer an additional fillip. These little touches lend distinction
to our service, scoring heavily in the aggregate."*

# red rider sundae

A popular fictional cowboy from the 1940s, *Red Ryder* was created by Stephen Slesinger and drawn by artist Fred Harman. Beginning Sunday, November 6, 1938, *Red Ryder* was syndicated by Newspaper Enterprise Association, eventually expanding to over 750 newspapers with a readership of 14 million in America. To avoid paying royalties to Slesinger, soda fountain operators changed the spelling of the reverential sundae to "Red Rider."

**2 scoops** vanilla ice cream
**3 tablespoons** chopped cherries
whipped cream
maraschino cherry

Into a tulip sundae glass put 1 tablespoon of chopped cherries. Add 2 scoops of vanilla ice cream. Cover with remaining chopped cherries. Top with whipped cream and garnish with cherry.

The popularity of *Red Ryder* spawned radio programs, events, rodeos, powwows, commercial tie-ins and licensed products such as the Daisy Red Ryder BB Gun.

*The maraschino cherry originated in northern Italy where merchants added a liqueur to a local cherry variety called the "marasca." By 1890 the delicacy was being imported into the United States, and it was this candied cherry that first appeared at the top of sundaes.*

# rocky road sundae

While 1929 may be remembered in American history as the year of the Stock Market Crash and the beginning of the Great Depression, ice cream enthusiasts may recall it as the year someone put sundae toppings inside of ice cream. Rocky Road ice cream was created by William Dreyer, founder of Dreyer's Ice Cream in Oakland, California. The ice cream's three components, chocolate ice cream, tiny marshmallows and toasted almonds, offered a variation of an original sundae of the times.

**2 scoops** chocolate ice cream
**4 ounces** marshmallow syrup
**1 teaspoon** broken macaroons
**1 teaspoon** pecans, chopped
**1 teaspoon** walnuts, chopped
maraschino cherry

Into a tulip sundae glass put 1 ounce marshmallow. Add 2 scoops of chocolate ice cream. Cover with remaining marshmallow syrup. Sprinkle macaroons, pecans, and walnuts over the top and garnish with cherry.

Some say the ice cream flavor was originally invented at Fenton's Creamery (also in Oakland), made with chopped candy bars including chocolate, walnuts and marshmallows among the ingredients.

*Dreyer's claims its founder named the Depression-era ice cream "Rocky Road" as an allusion to the economic rough road ahead.*

# scotch and fudge

For many years, the Howard Johnson name was part of American popular culture. It all started in 1925, at a small corner drugstore across from the Wollaston railroad station in Quincy, Massachusetts. Young Mr. Johnson discovered that the soda fountain was the most profitable part of his venture, a consequence of the popularity of his butterfat-rich ice cream. He opened concession stands along area beaches, then opened the first of what would eventually become a chain of over 1,000 restaurants and over 500 motor lodges in 42 states and Canada. One of Howard Johnson's early sundaes featured twin scoops of ice cream, originally with vanilla ice cream, later with peppermint stick ice cream.

**2 scoops** vanilla ice cream
**3 ounces** hot fudge sauce
**3 ounces** hot butterscotch sauce
whipped cream
2 maraschino cherries

Dip scoops of vanilla ice cream side by side in an oval dish. Cover one scoop with hot fudge, cover the other with butterscotch. Top with whipped cream and garnish with cherries.

According to *White's Vest Pocket Sundae Formulary*, **a similar fountain formula was called the Fifty-Fifty Sundae.**

*Instructions on sundaes from the* Howard Johnson's Fountain Service Manual:
*"Place a #16 conical scoop of ice cream in a sundae dish.*
*(This should be well molded into the dish to keep it upright at all times)*
*and cover with proper amount of syrup, sauce or fruit."*

# scotch lassie

Joe Beerntsen worked as a candy maker in Green Bay, Chicago, and Milwaukee before opening his own confectionery in Manitowoc, Wisconsin. Still going strong, the charming candy shop and soda fountain, with a striped awning out front and handsome dark woodwork inside, is a refreshing step back into time. Slide into one of the original black walnut booths and dig into an expertly-made, two-sauce sundae called the Scotch Lassie.

**2 scoops** vanilla ice cream
**3 ounces** hot butterscotch
**2 ounces** marshmallow
whipped cream
pecans, chopped

Into a tulip sundae glass put 1 ounce hot butterscotch. Add 2 scoops of vanilla ice cream. Cover one side with remaining butterscotch, the other with the marshmallow. Top with whipped cream and sprinkle with chopped pecans.

Thin glass cups are always attractive and there are many fancy glasses that are used for serving fancy sundaes.

According to sundae lore, 19th century Manitowoc soda fountain operator George Giffy established the prescient policy of limiting sales of a yet-to-be-named ice cream concoction to a single day of the week (Sunday).

# smith college ice

Before "sundae" became a universally-accepted term, Timothy A. Brosnan, a soda jerk at Easton's Drugstore in Worcester, Massachusetts, called his ice cream concoctions "college ices." The novelty of ice cream, formed into a pyramid or cone shape, topped with walnuts and chocolate syrup, and served in a champagne coupe, became a favorite confection of the young women from nearby Smith College who frequented his fountain. Another version was a "fruited cream," a combination of vanilla ice cream and crushed fruit.

**2 scoops** vanilla ice cream
**4 ounces** chocolate syrup
walnuts, chopped

Into a champagne coupe put vanilla ice cream. Cover with chocolate syrup. Top with walnuts.

{ In a long-standing Smith College tradition, first-year students are treated to old-fashioned ice cream sundaes served up by the deans }

From The Pacific Drug Review (1920): "The sundae is blessed with many names and the New England college girl glibly asks for a 'college ice' and receives nothing but a sundae. There are other names — and under them all is hidden many a delicious frozen confection."

# snowball

In 1920s Baltimore, "Snowball" was the name for a cup of shaved ice with syrup, pieces of fruit, and marshmallow. During the Great Depression, the Snowball sold for a penny and was known as "the hard-times sundae." In better years, Snowball was the name bestowed on a favorite restaurant dessert with vanilla ice cream rolled in coconut and topped with hot fudge. No lesser an institution than New York City's legendary Stork Club featured a sundae-style Snowball on its menu in the 1940s.

**1 scoop** vanilla ice cream
**1/2 cup** shredded coconut
**4 ounces** hot fudge sauce

Shape vanilla ice cream into a ball and place into the freezer for about 5 to 10 minutes. Pour the coconut onto a plate. Remove ice cream from the freezer and roll in the coconut. Return to a serving dish. Cover with hot fudge.

{ From its inception in the Roaring Twenties as a speakeasy to its heyday in the 50's, everyone from Marilyn Monroe to J. Edgar Hoover gathered at the Stork Club. }

In the 1946 film classic, It's a Wonderful Life, Mary Hatch declared her undying love for young George Bailey at the soda fountain of Gower's drugstore. She whispered her sentiments in George's deaf ear while he prepared her a sundae with coconut sprinkles from the Fiji Islands.

# soap box derby sundae

Originally, soapbox cars were built from wooden soap (or orange) crates and rollerskate wheels, unpowered, relying completely upon gravity to move. In 1933, *Dayton Daily News* newspaper photographer Myron Scott covered a race of boy-built cars in his home community and was so taken with the idea that he acquired rights to the event. In 1934, Scott managed to persuade fifty cities across the United States to hold soap box car races and send a champion each to Dayton for a major race, the birth of the national-scale Soap Box Derby and the inspiration for an ice cream sundae.

**2 scoops** chocolate ice cream
**4 ounces** marshmallow syrup
**4** Oreo cookies

Dip scoops of chocolate ice cream side by side in an oval dish. Cover with marshmallow. On the sides of the ice cream scoops place the four cookies (to represent wheels).

From *The Spatula* (1915): "Marshmallow can be used to advantage for topping fancy drinks, hot chocolate, etc.; and will be found very useful to every one who sells ice cream or dispenses soda water."

From American Druggist and Pharmaceutical Record (1906):
"The drug store window is one of the best mediums for advertising the soda fountain, and in window advertising, as a general rule, one is limited to window cards. Make them as attractive as possible."

# strawanna

A trip to Rumpelmayer's, that fabled pink ice cream parlor in the St. Moritz Hotel, was a New York holiday ritual for young girls, dressed delectably, with their festive coats and scarves and hats. The well-bred institution was famous for its marble soda fountain, pink décor, stuffed teddy bears, and sundaes of undiluted quality: the best ice cream, real whipped cream, superior fruit toppings, and French fan biscuits. Rumpelmayer's Strawanna sundae, made with fresh, ripe strawberries, was proper and restrained..

**1 scoop** strawberry ice cream
**1 scoop** vanilla ice cream
**3 tablespoons** crushed strawberries
**1/2** banana, peeled, sliced into wheels
whipped cream
whole fresh strawberry

Into a tulip sundae glass put 1 tablespoon crushed strawberries. Add 1 scoop strawberry and 1 scoop vanilla ice cream. Cover with remaining crushed strawberries. Top with whipped cream and garnish with whole strawberry.

From *The New York Times* (2003): "Rumpelmayer's enjoyed a long run at the center of New York's hot chocolate universe, but it closed several years ago — more a victim of age and exhaustion than of a nation's changing tastes."

New York's legendary soda jerk, Mr. Jennings, served behind the fountain of an ice cream parlor called Hicks for 26 years, creating fruit-laced flaming and hot fudge extravaganzas. He once said: "First God created heaven and earth. Then he created soda fountains."

# thanksgiving day sundae

*The Dispenser's Soda Water Guide*, published in 1909, encourages soda fountain managers to develop original recipes for "palatetickling concoctions." Special sundaes, it explains, are similar to sheet music – "they make a hit, no one knows why, and are profitable until the fad or craving for them is worn off." The creamy white pignoli nut lends its sweet, rich flavor to the passing fancy of a holiday-inspired sundae.

> **1 scoop** vanilla ice cream
> **1 scoop** chocolate ice cream
> **4 ounces** chocolate syrup
> walnuts, chopped
> pignoli nuts
> **2** maraschino cherries

Dip one scoop of vanilla ice cream and one scoop of chocolate ice cream side by side on an oval dish. Cover with chocolate syrup. Sprinkle pignoli nuts over the vanilla ice cream, walnuts over the chocolate. Garnish with cherries.

{ From *Let's Sell Ice Cream* (1947): "The chocolate sundae is the most asked for sundae at the soda fountain. There are enough variations to suit all tastes." }

From The Bulletin of Pharmacy (1917): "The value of appearance can be seen in the fact that the same ingredients that bring ten or fifteen cents in a plain sundae cup will bring from fifteen to twenty-five cents when served in a fancystem glass in a little different form."

# three graces

Before she became a showgirl, legendary comedienne Lucille Ball worked behind the soda fountain at her hometown (Jamestown, New York) Walgreen's drugstore. She claimed she was fired by the manager when she forgot to put the banana in a customer's banana split. Without the base of tropical fruit, think of Three Graces as a banana split minus the banana.

**1 scoop** vanilla ice cream
**1 scoop** chocolate ice cream
**1 scoop** strawberry ice cream
**2 tablespoons** crushed pineapple
**3 ounces** chocolate syrup
**2 tablespoons** crushed strawberries
whipped cream
walnuts, chopped
**3** maraschino cherries

Into an oval dish, add scoops of vanilla, chocolate, and strawberry ice creams. Cover vanilla ice cream with the crushed pineapple, chocolate ice cream with the chocolate syrup, and strawberry ice cream with the crushed strawberries. Top with whipped cream, sprinkle with chopped nuts, and garnish with cherries.

> According to *White's Vest Pocket Sundae Formulary*, a similar fountain formula was called the Three-in-One Sundae or a Musical Comedy.

*In a paradigm shift employed at some fountains, chopped peaches were substituted for chocolate syrup over the chocolate ice cream, and the sundae was called a Brunswick Delight; when chopped cherries were substituted for crushed pineapple over the vanilla ice cream, the sundae became a Maiden's Prayer.*

# tin roof sundae

In 1908 John E. Wirt, a young pharmacist working at the A.R. Keep drugstore in Meadville, Pennsylvania, decided that chocolate syrup and salted peanuts over a scoop of ice cream in a glass would attract more business to the store's soda fountain. He already knew that when salt and sweet are simultaneously applied to the tongue, each sensation is enhanced by the other. Wirt christened his creation the "tin roof," although over the years some have insisted on renaming the sundae a "Mexican."

**2 scoops** vanilla ice cream
**4 ounces** chocolate syrup
**1/3 cup** salted peanuts, whole

Into a tulip sundae glass put 1 ounce of the chocolate syrup. Add the vanilla ice cream. Cover with remaining chocolate syrup. Top with a layer of peanuts.

Salted Spanish peanuts are recommended for this dish, though chocolate syrup also teams beautifully with any other nut combination.

*Howard Lake Drug, one of the oldest drug stores in Minnesota, still has the original tin ceiling and counter fixtures. The seven-stool soda fountain features a Midwest version of the Tin Roof Sundae called the "Mudball."*

# tune-in sundae

Radio, though a reality in the late 1800s, didn't make a significant mark on the world until the 1920s. Considered the "Golden Age of Radio," a lot was happening in the 1930s, and America tuned in to keep in touch. Imagination of the listener was the key to radio, and imagination at the soda fountain was responsible for a radioinspired sundae.

**1 slice** vanilla ice cream brick
**3 ounces** marshmallow syrup
**3** chocolate bon bons
whipped cream, colored brown
with chocolate syrup

On a round, flat dish, place 1 slice of brick ice cream onto the center and cover with the marshmallow. On top, place the 3 bon bons at regular intervals (to represent the 3 dials of a radio). With brown colored whipped cream draw small lines from each chocolate center (in the manner of an indicator).

With a weekly radio broadcast, Duke Ellington and his band thrived in the period from 1932 to 1942, performing numbers such as the "Soda Fountain Rag."

From The Meyer Druggist (1921): "Specialty articles, especially at the soda fountain, may be sold at a good profit. It is not a matter of pricing the article. The secret lies in causing people to want it regardless of the price. Not only does a specialty article pay for the sales it brings for itself but it is equally valuable to draw people into the store where they are sure to make other purchases."

# turtle sundae

The turtle candy was first offered to the public in the early 1920s by Chicago confectioner Rowntree DeMet. An employee at the chocolate factory remarked that a new treat, chocolate-coated caramel with pecans protruding from its side, looked a lot like a turtle. The name stuck, and as the candy became a staple in the Midwest, it wasn't long before the marvelous combination of sweet, salty and creamy chocolate was embraced at ice cream parlors and a new sundae was born.

**2 scoops** chocolate ice cream
**3 ounces** chocolate syrup
**3 ounces** caramel syrup
whipped cream
pecans, chopped

Into a tulip sundae glass put 1 ounce chocolate and 1 ounce caramel syrups. Add 2 scoops of chocolate ice cream. Cover with remaining chocolate and caramel syrups. Top with whipped cream and sprinkle with the pecans.

Toasting the nuts creates a deeper and richer flavor, and add a dash of salt, always a good counterpoint to sweet.

*The Turtle Sundae is a miracle of synergy in the hands of gifted fountaineers, as cohabiting sauces assume the elegance of perfect poetry.*

# twin peaks sundae

Long before David Lynch's cult TV series of the same name, a two-scoop sundae was named for San Francisco's Twin Peaks, the two hills situated at the geographic center of the city and a prominent divider for the summer coastal fog pushed in from the Pacific Ocean. Due to this unique geographical condition, their westfacing slopes generally receive substantial fog and strong winds, while the east-facing slopes usually receive more sun and warmth.

**2 scoops** vanilla ice cream
**4 ounces** chocolate syrup
whipped cream
walnuts, chopped
**2** maraschino cherries

Dip two scoops of vanilla ice cream side by side on an oval dish. Cover each scoop with 2 ounces of chocolate syrup. Top each scoop with a sprinkle of walnuts, a dab of whipped cream and a cherry.

{ A similar version of the Twin Peaks Sundae is served at San Francisco's legendary Ghirardelli's, topped with a dense whipped cream "fog." }

*In the film, Tea with Mussolini, Maggie Smith portrays Lady Hester Random, a quintessential English snob. Anything that doesn't conform to her notion of propriety becomes subject to her scorn. Observing a sundae being served, she sniffs that Americans have even found a way to "vulgarize ice cream."*

# two on a blanket

It was Portland, Oregon, in 1963, where Bob Farrell opened the first of what would become a chain of ice cream "parlours," recreating a segment of one of the most colorful and memorable eras in American history – the Gay Nineties. If it was your birthday, sirens wailed as a sundae was delivered to your table, free of charge! "Two on a Blanket" was a pound cake-based Farrell's original, featuring the yin and yan of vanilla and chocolate.

> **1 scoop** vanilla ice cream
> **1 scoop** chocolate ice cream
> **4 ounces** hot fudge sauce
> **4 ounces** marshmallow syrup
> **1 slice** pound cake
> mixed nuts, chopped
> **2** maraschino cherries

Place one large scoop each of vanilla and chocolate ice cream side by side on a slice of toasted pound cake. Cover the vanilla ice cream with hot fudge and chocolate with marshmallow. Top with whipped cream, sprinkle with the chopped mixed nuts, and garnish with cherries.

{ From Emily Post's *Advice for Every Dining Occasion*: "Ice cream is generally eaten with a spoon, but when accompanied by cake, either the spoon alone or both the spoon and fork may be used." }

*The logo which adorned Farrell's menus and advertisements had its roots in the works of Charles Dana Gibson. His creation of the "Gibson Girl" became the foundation for most of his paintings during the early 20th century.*

# uncle sam sundae

One of St. Louis' oldest and most popular attractions, Crown Candy Kitchen was opened in 1913 by Harry Karandzieff and Pete Jugaloff, who brought their confectionary skills from Greece. During the early 1950s Harry's son George took over, determined to maintain sundae categories long since vanished from most American fountains: A sundae is ice cream and syrup; a "Newport" includes whipped cream and nuts; a "Deluxe" adds more flavors of ice cream and/or syrups.

**2 scoops** vanilla ice cream
**3 ounces** crushed strawberries
**3 ounces** crushed pineapple
**1** banana, peeled, sliced into wheels
whipped cream
jimmies (red, white & blue)
**2** maraschino cherries

Dip 2 scoops of vanilla ice cream side by side in an oval dish. Cover one scoop with the crushed strawberries, the other scoop with the crushed pineapple. Surround the ice cream with banana wheels. Top with whipped cream, sprinkle with jimmies, and garnish with cherries.

{
In Missouri, the ice cream sundae is pronounced "sunduh."
According to the locals, "Sunday" is the day you go to church,
and a "sunduh" is what you eat after you go to church.
}

From The American Druggist and Pharmaceutical Record (1916):
"The pharmacist usually experiences little difficulty in devising new sundaes and names, the chief difficulty being connected with the improvement of the older popular formulas."

# valentine sundae

By 1929, sixty percent of America's 58,258 drugstores had installed soda fountains, as the fountain became the most popular public gathering place. It was here that many a young man used the opportunity to woo the pretty young girls with ice cream sundaes. The gee-whiz, double-scoop Valentine Sundae, a popular 1920s offering, was served with two spoons to encourage sharing – and romance.

> **2 scoops** strawberry ice cream
> **4 ounces** marshmallow syrup
> whipped cream
> small candy red heart

Into a tulip sundae glass put 1 ounce marshmallow syrup. Add 1 scoop of strawberry ice cream, and cover with 1 ounce marshmallow syrup. Add the second scoop of strawberry ice cream, and cover with remaining marshmallow. Top with whipped cream and place the candy red heart at the center.

From *The Pacific Drug Review* (1920): "Sundae cups (they may be glass or silver) should be dainty and severely plain, so that they can be kept clean without much trouble."

*Around the beginning of the 20th century, Somerville, Massachusetts resident, Archibald Query, invented marshmallow creme. He soon afterward sold the recipe to two candymakers, H. Allen Durkee and Fred Mower, for $500. In 1917, the product first hit supermarket shelves in cans as Toot Sweet Marshmallow Fluff.*

# vanilla poached eggs on toast

Back in the 1940s, a soda jerk by the name of Jean Gude invented the "Fried Egg Sundae," served ever since at the fountain of Stoner Drug in Hamburg, Iowa. In its center is a scoop of cream-colored vanilla ice cream covered with marshmallow, which could be construed to resemble the yolk of an easy-over egg, and it is ringed with chocolate syrup to suggest the browned edges of the white. "Vanilla Poached Eggs on Toast" was another mimic of the breakfast menu offered during the heyday of the soda fountain.

**1 scoop** vanilla ice cream, softened
**1 slice** sponge cake
**1/2** peach (or apricot), pitted

Cut sponge cake to resemble a slice of toast and spread a thin layer of the vanilla ice cream on top to resemble the white of an egg. Place half a peach or an apricot on top, round side up to resemble the yolk.

From *The Pacific Drug Review* (1920): "The finest concoction loses its charm if indifferently served."

*According to Paul Dickson in* The Great American Ice Cream Book *(1972), "Lagging Depression-era sales prompted the industry to unveil a variety of bizarre 'sales-stimulating' ice cream combinations and do-it-yourself suggestions like this one."*

# waldorf sundae

A traditional Waldorf Salad consists of apples, walnuts, celery, and a mayonnaise-based dressing. The salad was created by Oscar Tschirky, the maitre d' hotel at New York's Waldorf Astoria Hotel for a private party on the pre-opening of the hotel on March 13, 1893. By the 1930s, the Cole Porter musical *Anything Goes* featured a song ("You're the Top") that makes a reference to it with the line: "You're the top, you're a Waldorf Salad." The popularity of the restaurant salad did not go unnoticed at the soda fountain, and was eventually re-invented as a sundae.

**2 scoops vanilla ice cream**
**1 tablespoon** apple, peeled, coarsely-chopped
**1 tablespoon** walnuts, chopped
whipped cream
**2** maraschino cherries

Dip scoops of ice cream side by side in an oval dish. In the center between the two, place a mixture of the apple and walnuts. Top with whipped cream and garnish with cherries.

{ The formula for a "Waldorf Parfait" alternates layers of vanilla ice cream with crushed pineapple, crushed raspberries, chopped nuts, whipped cream and cherry. }

*Making things look nice at a clean fountain where the dispenser has good materials to work with is a matter of dexterity. Of course he must have thin, dainty glasses, etc., because you know that a drink looks better and tastes better when served in a thin glass than when served in a thick one.*

# white's flyer

In the introduction to *The Soda Water Guide and Book of Tested Recipes* (1910), the Liquid Carbonic Company, a manufacturer of soda fountains and fountain, explained: "In this book we have sought to embody important facts and helpful information that years of experience in the trade have given us. No effort or expense has been spared to make the book of practical daily usefulness to the dispenser." Entries included the White's Flyer.

**1 scoop** vanilla ice cream
**1/2 ounce** vanilla extract
**1 ounce** sweet cream
**1** egg
whipped cream
maraschino cherry

Dip 1 scoop of vanilla ice cream into a tulip sundae glass. In a separate glass, mix the vanilla syrup, cream and egg. Shake well and pour over the ice cream. Top with whipped cream and garnish with cherry.

DISPENSING TIP: Break the egg into the glass first before adding any other ingredients.

*The tradition of soda fountain slang, used by waiters in calling their order to soda fountain men, included a call to "break it and shake it," instruction to crack an egg and add it to a drink or the topping for a sundae.*

# zombie

The abundant joys of frozen custard have to do with formulation and method of production. Its thick, creamy texture and smooth consistency is achieved in machines that churn slowly instead of whipping, incorporating less air or "overrun" than traditional ice cream. Since 1938, when Paul Gilles opened a small stand on Bluemound Road, frozen custard has been a Wisconsin staple and a Milwaukee specialty, defining the place and shaping a substantial part of its culture. No wonder a cult following lines up at Gilles for Zombies, even on the coldest winter days.

**3 scoops** vanilla frozen custard
**1** banana, peeled, sliced into wheels
**3 ounces** hot fudge
**2 tablespoons** crushed pineapple
**2 tablespoons** crushed strawberries
walnuts, chopped
whipped cream
chocolate jimmies
**3** maraschino cherries

Dip 3 scoops of frozen vanilla custard side by side on a banana split dish. Arrange banana wheels around the custard. Cover one scoop with hot fudge, one with crushed pineapple and one with crushed strawberries. Top each scoop with a sprinkle of walnuts, a dab of whipped cream and a cherry.

*The white caps worn by soda jerks in American pharmacies and ice cream parlors in the 1930s and 1940s were inspired by military apparel, to create a sense of authority and to clearly indicate who was in charge.*

# addendum

# vanilla ice cream

**2** eggs
**1 can (14 ounces)** sweetened condensed milk
**1/4 cup** sugar
**1/4 cup** brown sugar
**2 cups** heavy cream
**2 cups** half & half
**2 1/2 tablespoons** pure vanilla extract
pinch of salt

In a large mixing bowl, whisk eggs, add condensed milk and whisk together until thoroughly mixed. Add sugar and brown sugar and again mix thoroughly. Then add heavy cream, half and half, a pinch of salt and vanilla extract. Let the mix chill in the refrigerator for about four hours, which allows the mixture to age. Pour into an ice cream canister and freeze, following the directions of your ice cream-making machine. **Makes 1 1/2 quarts**

# chocolate ice cream

**2** eggs
**1 can (14 ounces)** sweetened condensed milk
**1/4 cup** sugar
**2 cups** heavy cream
**1 1/2 cups** half & half
**2/3 cup** chocolate syrup
pinch of salt

In a large mixing bowl, whisk eggs, add condensed milk and whisk together until thoroughly mixed. Add sugar and brown sugar and again mix thoroughly. Then add heavy cream, half and half, a pinch of salt and vanilla extract. Let the mix chill in the refrigerator for about four hours, which allows the mixture to age. Pour into an ice cream canister and freeze, following the directions of your ice cream-making machine. **Makes 1 1/2 quarts**

# strawberry ice cream

**1 1/2 quarts** Vanilla Ice Cream mixture
(refrigerated for 4 hours)
**2 pints** fresh, ripe strawberries
**1/2** cup sugar
**1/2** lemon

Clean and top the strawberries and cut them into bite-sized pieces.
Add sugar and the juice of the half lemon. Let strawberries marinate in the
refrigerator overnight or at least 4 hours. When the Vanilla Ice Cream mix
has been sufficiently chilled and is ready for use, strain the strawberries,
reserving the juice. Place the strawberries in the freezer compartment of
your refrigerator. Combine the strawberry syrup and vanilla cream. Freeze
the ice cream mix, following the rules of your ice cream maker. When the
ice cream is almost frozen, add the strawberries and finish freezing.

# chocolate syrup

**6 ounces** semi-sweet chocolate
**1/2 cup** evaporated milk
**1/4 cup** water

Melt chocolate in top of a double boiler. Gradually stir in evaporated milk,
and continue stirring until sauce is fully blended and smooth. Remove
from heat and stir in water until smooth.

Note: Syrup may be refrigerated in an airtight container for up to 3 weeks.
To reheat, set over a double boiler and stir until smooth. If re-heating over
direct heat, use very low flame, and be careful not to let the sauce bubble
or burn. **Makes 1 cup**

# caramel syrup

**1 cup** granulated sugar
**1/3 cup** water
**1 cup** heavy cream

Combine sugar and water in a heavy medium-size saucepan. Stir constantly over medium heat until sugar is dissolved and the mixture comes to a boil. Stop stirring and boil until the mixture turns a deep caramel color (6-12 minutes). Watch carefully to make sure mixture doesn't get too dark. Remove from heat and add cream (caution: mixture will bubble up fiercely). Return pan to high heat and boil, stirring occasionally, for 2 minutes. Remove from heat and pour into a glass measuring cup or other heatproof container. Allow to cool to desired temperature. Syrup can be refrigerated in an airtight container for up to 3 weeks. To reheat, microwave on low power at 15-second intervals, or until warm. **Makes 1 cup**

# coffee syrup

**1 cup** sugar
**1 cup** extra strength brewed coffee

Combine sugar and coffee in a medium saucepan. Bring to a boil, stirring constantly to dissolve sugar. Lower heat and simmer for three minutes, stirring often. **Makes 1 cup**

# melba syrup

**1 cup** fresh raspberries
1/4 cup sugar

Force raspberries through a sieve fine enough to hold back the seeds.
Place into a sauce pan, add sugar and cook over moderate heat for 10
minutes, or long enough to make a heavy syrup. Serve cold.
**Makes 1/2 cup**

# hot fudge

**1 tablespoon** unsweetened cocoa powder
**1 cup** sugar
**3/4 cup** heavy cream
**1/4 cup** light corn syrup
**2 tablespoons** unsalted butter
**2 ounces** unsweetened chocolate, chopped
**1 teaspoon** vanilla extract
Pinch of salt
Few drops of malt vinegar

In a heavy medium saucepan over medium heat, whisk together the cocoa,
sugar, and 1/4 cup of the heavy cream until smooth, about 2 minutes.
Stir in the corn syrup, butter, unsweetened chocolate bits and remaining
1/2 cup heavy cream, and bring to a boil. Remove from the heat and stir
in the vanilla, salt and vinegar.

Note: Sauce may be refrigerated in an airtight container for up to 3 weeks.
To reheat, set over a double boiler, whisking vigorously. If re-heating over
direct heat, use very low flame, and be careful not to let the sauce bubble
or burn. **Makes 2 cups**

# claret syrup

**1 cup** sugar
**1/4 cup** water
**1/3 cup** red wine

Boil sugar and water eight minutes; cool slightly, and add claret. **Makes 1/2 cup**

# hot butterscotch

**1/4 cup** water
**1 cup** sugar
**6 tablespoons** unsalted butter, cut up
**1 cup** heavy cream
**1/2 cup** sweetened condensed milk
**2 tablespoons** unsalted butter (for browning)

In a medium saucepan, combine water and sugar over medium heat but do not stir. The sugar will melt and the mixture will come to a boil. Watch it carefully, using a pastry brush to wash down the crystals from the sides of the pan, until the mixture turns a deep amber color. Add the 6 tablespoons butter and stir over low heat. Add heavy cream and stir well, then add the condensed milk and stir once more. Bring to a boil and let the mixture bubble for 2 minutes. Remove from the heat. In a small saucepan, cook the 2 tablespoons butter until it foams and browns. Whisk the butter into the sauce. Warm the sauce over low heat before spooning it onto a sundae. **Makes 2 cups**

# hot penuche

1/4 cup light corn syrup
1 cup tightly packed dark brown sugar
3/4 cup heavy cream
1 teaspoon vanilla extract
1/2 teaspoon kosher salt

In a 2 quart saucepan, heat corn syrup over low to medium heat. Gradually add dark brown sugar, stirring with wooden spoon until sugar is uniformly wet. Stir occasionally until mixture goes from looking grainy to molten lava. Add the heavy cream and replace your spoon with a whisk. Lower heat a little and whisk cream into mixture. When liquid is uniform, turn heat back to medium and whisk every few minutes for a total of 10 minutes. After liquid has been boiling on the stove for its 10 minutes, turn heat off and let rest for a minute or two before transferring into a stainless steel or glass bowl. Whisk in salt and vanilla extract. **Makes 1 1/2 cup**

# brownies

1/4 cups semi-sweet chocolate
1 pound (4 sticks) butter
3 cups granulated sugar
1 cup cake flour
1 tablespoon baking powder
4 whole eggs
2 cups crushed walnuts

Preheat the oven to 300 degrees. Melt the chocolate with the butter in a double boiler. Mix the sugar, flour and baking powder together in a bowl. Mix the chocolate with the flour mixture, about 4 to 5 minutes. Add the eggs and mix. Pour the mixture into a 9-by-13-inch baking pan. Sprinkle the walnuts on top, pressing the walnuts down slightly into the mixture with your hand. Bake for 30 to 40 minutes. After removing from the oven, allow to cool about 30 minutes.

**Makes 24 servings**

# roasted almonds

**1 cup** fresh almonds
**1 tablespoon** extra-virgin olive oil
**1/2 teaspoon** sea salt

Place almonds in a single layer on flat pan or cookie sheet. Add the oil
and toss to coat evenly. Roast in a pre-heated 325-degree oven for 20
to 30 minutes, stirring occasionally. Remove from oven and sprinkle with
salt. **Makes 1 cup**

# wet walnuts

**3/4 cup** corn syrup
**1/2 cup** pure maple syrup
**1/2 cup** granulated sugar
**1/4 cup** water
**1 1/4 cups** coarsely chopped walnuts

In a saucepan, combine the corn syrup, maple syrup, sugar and water
and place it over medium heat. Bring to a boil, stirring occasionally.

Stir in the nuts, reduce the heat and simmer uncovered for about 25
minutes or until thick. **Makes 2 cups**

# hot chocolate shell

**6 ounces** chopped dark chocolate
(either bittersweet or semi-sweet),
**1 stick (1/4 pound)** salted butter
**1/2 cup** walnuts, coarsely chopped (optional)

In a small saucepan, over low heat, melt the chocolate with the butter, stirring constantly. If desired, add walnuts. Keep warm, just melted, not hot.

To coat ice cream in a cone, slowly spoon the sauce over the ball of ice cream, twirling the cone as you go. Make sure the ice cream is very hard. For a sundae, place a scoop of very hard ice cream in a long stemmed glass. Spoon chocolate sauce on top. **Makes 1 cup**

# strawberry topping

**2 quarts** fresh, sweet strawberries
**1 cup** sugar (a little more if berries are tart)

Wash, stem and crush berries, using a potato masher or fork, and crust lightly with sugar. Let set for at least an hour to allow berries to macerate and release their juice. Transfer sweetened berries and juice to a large, heavy saucepan and carefully bring to a simmer. Cook, stirring often, for about 12 to 15 minutes or until slightly thickened.

# marshmallow topping

**2** large egg whites
**1 cup** sugar
**1/2 cup** water
**16** regular marshmallows
**1/4 teaspoon** vanilla extract

Using an electric mixer, beat egg whites in a mixing bowl on medium speed until soft peaks form, about 2-3 minutes. Set aside. Combine sugar and water in a medium-size saucepan and place over medium heat. Stir until sugar dissolves. Stop stirring and allow sugar/water mixture to come to a boil. Boil for 3 minutes without stirring. Reduce heat to low, add marshmallows, and stir until they are completely melted and mixture is smooth, about 4 minutes. Remove from heat and, using the electric mixer on low speed, beat hot marshmallow mixture into the egg whites. Continue beating for 2 minutes. Beat in vanilla. Serve warm or cold.

Note: Sauce may be refrigerated in an airtight container for up to 3 weeks. To re-heat, microwave on low power for 30 seconds, or until warm. Makes 3 cups

# whipped cream

**1 cup** heavy cream
**1/4 cup** sweetened condensed milk

Combine heavy whipping cream and condensed milk (both wellchilled) in a metal mixing bowl. Whip with a hand-held electric mixer at medium-high speed. To incorporate the most air, move the beaters up, down, and around the sides of the bowl during whipping. When the cream has doubled in volume and forms stiff peaks, you are ready to a dramatic swirl to a sundae. Note: The richer the cream, the more air it will trap and hold. Most recipes call for confectioner's sugar, but sweetened condensed milk makes a more stable whipped cream.

# memorandum

120

# about the author

Michael Turback's intellectually rich reflections have added surprising, entertaining dimensions to the culinary landscape. *In A Month of Sundaes* he takes readers on a 30-chapter journey through the history and folklore of the Ice Cream Sundae; a follow-up work, *The Banana Split Book*, trains a microscopic eye on the origins of the iconic dessert and its status in the social chronicle of an entire century; *Greetings from the Finger Lakes: A Food and Wine Lover's Companion* celebrates achievements in winemaking, artisan farming, and culinary invention; *Hot Chocolate* features 60 trendsetting recipes contributed by the world's preeminent chocolatiers; *Mocha* explores the partnership of chocolate and coffee in a range of original drinks and desserts from chocolatiers, pastry chefs, and baristas. *Coffee Drinks* introduces imaginative recipes for espresso based beverages, custom-crafted in national and international barista competitions. The author lives and works in the enlightened city of Ithaca, New York, birthplace of the ice cream sundae.